Rip the Labels Off

Don't Allow Society to Define Who You Were Created to Be

Ryda Isabella Percy

abbott press

This book is a work of non-fiction. Unless otherwise noted, the author and the publisher make no explicit guarantees as to the accuracy of the information contained in this book and in some cases, names of people and places have been altered to protect their privacy.

Scripture quotations are taken from the KING JAMES VERSION (KJV), public domain.

Abbott Press books may be ordered through booksellers or by contacting:

Abbott Press
1663 Liberty Drive
Bloomington, IN 47403
www.abbottpress.com
Phone: 1 (866) 697-5310

Because of the dynamic nature of the Internet, any web addresses or links contained in this book may have changed since publication and may no longer be valid. The views expressed in this work are solely those of the author and do not necessarily reflect the views of the publisher, and the publisher hereby disclaims any responsibility for them.

Any people depicted in stock imagery provided by Getty Images are models, and such images are being used for illustrative purposes only. Certain stock imagery © Getty Images.

ISBN: 978-1-4582-2186-5 (sc)
ISBN: 978-1-4582-2185-8 (hc)
ISBN: 978-1-4582-2184-1 (e)

Library of Congress Control Number: 2018907560

Print information available on the last page.

Abbott Press rev. date: 07/06/2018

Contents

DEDICATION

This book is dedicated to every person who has been
heartbroken, abused, angry, depressed, has battled with low
self-esteem, failed, cried and wanted to give up. Although
those labels chased you down and attached themselves to you,
God sees you as someone who makes a difference in the world,
someone who matters, and someone who has purpose.
You can make it.

PREFACE

Everything that has happened to us, every label applied to us that we've accepted as true, all started with a root.

My labels started with rejection. As a child not understanding why my father didn't want me and wondering why we had to go live with my aunt. Never feeling like I was wanted by the people who created me, would make anyone feel as though they were an orphan. The root of rejection continued into my adult life and has affected me in more ways than one. Rejection has prevented me from applying for positions and reaching out to try to become part of other people's lives, and groups because I was afraid of the rejection I would possibly hear in their response.

I have learned that if we don't figure out the root of the labels placed on us, they will continue to grow. This includes labels that grow as offshoots from the root of your label. It may be painful, but we must find a way to remove the dirt and revisit the root, so we can be free from a control that consumes us and blocks us from our destiny. My question to you is what is the root that is causing your other labels to produce and grow?

There is one positive about being labeled. It allows God to show us that He's all powerful, and only He can clean us up with no residue left behind. If you have ever ripped a label off of something, you know there is always that sticky, glue-like residue left behind that you have to work to get off. Once we accept that the negative label has to go, that's when God comes in and cleans off even the residue of that thing. Many people see the *post* us, but not the *pre*, when we were sticky and gross. We must allow Jesus to help us, and when He does, people who knew you before won't even recognize you. It's one of the most common clichés out, but it's so true. When God rips the labels off,

We won't look like what we've been through!

Acknowledgements

I would like to thank everyone who has assisted me in my ripping process: My family, friends, pastors, church families, haters, strangers, and labelers. You all are the authors of this book, I'm just the narrator Jesus used to tell the story. I've learned from each and every one of you what to do, what *not* to do, and how to love past what the label says. Thank you for pushing me, preying on me, believing in me, and last but not least, praying for me.

INTRODUCTION

For most of our lives we have been labeled by what society thinks about us and when people agree with them, we tend to believe it. Labels are placed on us because of our lack of confidence in who we are and what we were created to be. Think about it, there is no way someone should be able to tell the sun that it is a cloud. The sun knows its purpose and has been bringing light, warming, and even putting smiles on people's faces for thousands of years. The sun is confident in its ability to do the job it was created to do. Regardless of what happens, the sun will shine. You must have enough confidence to know that you don't have to answer to anything that anyone calls you other than your name and purpose. My life has not been all colorful and beautiful or stress free, but I am able to share my story with you because I've made it. I had so many people place bets on me that I wouldn't make it, but I am writing to say I did make it saved, sanctified, Holy Ghost filled, and in my right mind. There were many, many times that quitting sounded good and would have been easy, but the way Jesus ordained my life, quitting was not an option. I had to go through every phase of my life so someone else could know that success, sanctification, and salvation are possible, right, and necessary in order to make it.

Fifteen months prior to completing this book I had a God encounter. I was coming back from my second job and was dropping a student off at home, and I noticed a vehicle in the far right of the parking lot. The location of the vehicle made me take a second look, but I continued to gather my things. Right before I was going to get out, I looked again and saw a woman outside of the car praising Jesus in a dance, with her mouth and hands. This made my soul happy. I rolled down the window as I gathered my things and yelled, "You better praise Him!" I was going to park and go on in the building so the people would not think I was intruding on their praise session. But the Holy Spirit said to me, "Go over there." I was a little reluctant, but I obeyed what I was told. When I reached the SUV, I greeted the driver with, "Praise the Lord." She responded back, "Praise the Lord. Do you have a ministry?" I said, "No, I am actually looking for a church home." She said, "That's not what I asked you. I said, "Do you have a ministry?" From that point on, this complete stranger began to prophesy to me about every aspect of my life and what I was going through naturally and spiritually. One thing she said to me was, "When you yelled out of that window, God said He is going to use your voice to bring people into His Kingdom. The devil will try to silence you, but He won't be able to."

I knew what I was trying to do with my book and to prayerfully get some speaking engagements to tell my testimony in order to lead people to Jesus. My mind was blown, and I too had already begun to join in the full-fledged church service that was going on in that parking lot. Tears were rolling down my face and I began to speak in tongues as the Spirit of God gave utterance, and I waved my hands, telling Jesus thank you. Through much prayer and fasting, I am declaring that this book will be one of the ways that God will be able to use my voice all over the world to build His Kingdom.

The fact that you are reading this book, is a true testament to the fact that you have made it, despite being in the eye of the storm. I have been there. I have experienced many struggles, disappointments, and setbacks, but it wasn't until I learned who God is and who I am to Him, that my life finally became whole, even with all of the things spiritually, naturally, and physically that were missing from my life. WITH GOD IT IS POSSIBLE for you to achieve every dream, goal, and idea that you may have. When things are impossible for you, God says, I make everything POSSIBLE. We have to learn how to not accept the labels society has placed on us. We also have the horrible habit of placing labels on ourselves, and that is not healthy either. Some things I am sharing in detail I have never told anyone, except for you who are reading this. I share my story to help someone who is living on the edge—who feels they just can't make it—to give them hope.

"But ye are a CHOSEN generation, a royal priesthood, a holy nation, a peculiar people; that ye should shew forth the praises of him who hath called you out of darkness into his marvelous light" (1 Peter 2:9, KJV). This is the scripture that has always stood out to me. I knew I was chosen, and that Jesus has a special assignment for me to do what others would not be able to complete or refused to complete.

Ever since I was a little girl, I knew there was something different about me. I never fit in with any of my peers. I was always too dark, too fat, too loud, too poor, not smart enough … something prevented me from being "a part" of any group. The labels that were placed on me told me that I was always too much and never enough. Now that I am an adult, I understand that God CHOSE me not to fit in. Everything that is manufactured has a label on it and that is how you identify the product. What is the first thing you think of when you see the golden arches? I am pretty sure you immediately thought about McDonald's. The same applies when we think about ourselves. Whatever label is attached to us, that is how people identify who we are. No, it doesn't always feel good to be on the outside looking in, but when on the outside, you are able to see the entire picture, including the artist, and not just the finished product. There was always something abstract about the way I thought, felt, and acted that was different from other people. The important lesson in this is that the artist (God) always knows what color, how much pressure, and how long it will take for the finished masterpiece to be displayed.

The chapters in this book represent the many labels that over the years have attached themselves to my life. As you come with me on the journey of my life, you will see how with God, I was able to attempt to rip off each and every one. All of my labels have not came off, but many have and every day I work to rip and get rid of any residue.

LABEL 1

Rejection

Living in Cardinal, Kentucky, I had a wonderful relationship with my eldest aunt. My mother was a single, teen parent, and she lacked the adult skills to raise three children. In my heart, I knew she did the best she could. Sometimes my younger brother and I would be at my aunt's house for days not knowing when or if our mother was coming back to get us. We weren't old enough to do things for ourselves, so when we were young, it was best that our mother would send us somewhere where our needs could be met. My aunt had three older children who loved us as if we were one of them, so it was easy to stay. When my mother would come and get us, we never wanted to leave the normalcy that we had grown to appreciate with our aunt. Even though we were fragile, my aunt knew what we needed and how to tend to us even in the state we were in. My aunt did not have much, but she was not selfish with what she had and shared with my sibling and I. Aunt LaLa lived in an apartment complex called Tower Apartments. Once you parked in the parking lot, you had to walk down what seemed to be an outside hallway—a space between two tall buildings—to reach my aunt's apartment. She lived on the top floor on the left and could only be reached through the outside stairs.

I have few memories of my time in Cardinal because I was so young. One memory that I do have is of a man named Andrew. This man, who was tall and dark-complexed and wore his hair in an afro, came over and picked me up many times from the Tower Apartments. I enjoyed spending time with him, and he even told me that he was my father. He took me to get candy and ice cream and played games with me.

One day, out of the blue, he just stopped showing up, calling, and coming to see me. I always wondered what happened to the man that claimed we shared the same DNA. Did he get mad at my mother? Did my mother get mad at him, or did he just not love me anymore? How could a father leave his princess standing at the door waiting for his return for hours, which turned into days, which turned into weeks and eventually decades. I have always wondered if he thinks about me and wonders what kind of woman I have become.

Many times I have tried to find him; I had my cousin go to where I thought his sister's business was, but still no luck. I would have loved to continue a relationship with my father, but since he has never returned after so many years, that has never come to pass. Whenever I see fathers with their daughters, I still feel like something is missing in my life. Some people would use this as an excuse to be unproductive, miserable, or defeated. I use it as an excuse to be great and never give up on my goals and dreams.

There are many things about my personality that I don't see anywhere on my mother's side of the family, and I find that interesting. For example, I am a risk-taker. I will try something at least one time because even if I fail or lose, I at least learn a lesson. I believe the only way you fail is if you don't try. When you try, you don't lose because of the experiences that you gain. Depending on who you ask, I have lost many times, but that's the belief of someone who can only see the outside and not the heart of a determined leader. This is how the seed of rejection was first planted in me and began to take root.

My mother later married a man by the name of Dewayne; he was absolutely amazing and very talented. He would paint anything that he saw; I think houses were his favorite. My mother always seemed to be happy when she was with him, smiling and laughing all the time. Dewayne treated my mother like a woman should be treated, and most of all, he truly loved her and her children. Although they were happy together, one thing kept them from being together forever—his kidney disease. I am not sure what it was called, but he had to go to dialysis two to three times a week, and it was hard on him. Not long after, we moved into an apartment that looked like a two-story house, he became very sick. One night, he began to have an "attack". We didn't have a phone, so my mother knocked on all the doors in the building to get help, but no one answered. Knowing her husband needed help immediately, she went outside naked, thinking someone would call the police and that would lead to assistance for her fatally ill husband. This worked, believe it or not. Someone reported a woman running naked up and down the street, and that led to the ambulance taking him to the emergency room. I am not sure what happened the next couple of days in that hospital because my brother and I were too young to visit him in ICU. The last time we saw him alive was when the ambulance took him to the hospital. I believe my mother was so distraught over her young husband's death that she wanted a change. She decided that we should go back to Indiana, where she had grown up.

LABEL 2

Insecure

When you are insecure, you allow things to happen to you and you don't use your voice to defend yourself. Insecure people tend to tolerate a little more because they are not strong enough to stand up for themselves. My label of being insecure started in elementary school when I became intimidated and afraid. Sometimes even when we know right from wrong, we keep quiet because it can affect many other people outside of ourselves. Looking back, it was better for me to keep quiet and not say anything. Please, don't confuse my insecurities with defending what was wrong, but it kept things a little more peaceful in my home.

My little brother, my mother, and I moved to a small town in Indiana. I left my aunt's house thinking I was never going to see her again. I couldn't help wondering how things were going to end up. When we moved, I was in the first grade. I was nervous about going to a new school and having to meet new people, but my mother eased some of the pressure when she went school shopping for us. On the first day of school, I thought I was sharp as a tack. My hair was combed nicely, I had on a new outfit, and most of all, I had my Sheera shoes on, which I had waited weeks to wear. The school I went to was rather large, and a lot of the people there I had never seen before. As I entered the classroom, I said to myself, *I can do this*. Just then, Mrs. Washington greeted me and seated me at my desk. First grade was kind of difficult and took some adjusting to, but after being there for a couple of weeks, socializing became easy.

Every Friday we had a spelling test, and one day I took it upon myself to cheat. Education was not a priority in my house, so I felt like I had to do what I had to do. One girl that sat by me made A's on every single test. Here was my chance to get a good grade as well, I thought. I slouched down in my chair, repositioned my folder, put one hand over my eyebrows so I could see her paper, and before I knew it, there was Mrs. Washington tapping me on my shoulder and escorting me to the principal's office. I learned I had to study my words, so I could get a good grade. I was embarrassed by my actions and had to sit alone during any test thereafter. In the first grade, I began to make friends that would last through high school, but I did not feel as strong and as powerful they were.

In the beginning, I didn't think being in Indiana was going to work or be in our best interest. My Aunt Liz had been taking care of my older brother while we lived in Cardinal, so it was good being around him consistently. Once we started school and began to get familiar with our new life, it wasn't that bad. Aunt Liz always had a man over at the house who everyone called Uncle. He was not our real uncle; that was just his nickname. My aunt didn't drive, and her children were too young to drive, so he took her to pay bills, go grocery shopping, and run errands. At the time, my mother did not have her license either, so she called him to take her places as well. He was always nice and never minded helping out our family.

Later that year, both of my brothers and I began going to Uncle's house. Uncle lived out in the country on a gravel road about fifteen or twenty minutes away from town, so many times we fell asleep on the drive there. When you finally got to the gravel road and came over the railroad tracks, you could see only three houses sitting at the bottom of the steep hill. The first house belonged to one of his relatives, the second was his house, and the third was situated about a half mile down the road. Pulling onto his property, there was a small front yard with a big tree close to the edge of the road next to the mailbox. A small white house sat back from the road with a small lot for parking that was just dirt, no gravel. There were chickens with a chicken house diagonal from the house to the right. A small deep ditch ran behind the chicken house that we loved to play in. Beside the chicken house was a little dog house big enough for a medium sized dog. Uncle loved vehicles, old and new, trucks, antiques. He would get them and fix them up, many times selling them. At any given time, he would have three or four running vehicles that would be in the yard. Directly behind the house under a carport was a huge pile of coal for the heating stove.

When you first entered the house from the front door to the left was the kitchen area that was not used that much, but had snacks, bread, and crackers on the table. The refrigerator, a very small counter and cabinets with the sink were all on the left side. Next to the sink against the far wall was the washer that sat beside the side door. On the other side of the door was the stove and dryer. A huge floor model television was on the left with lots of papers, old mail, a VCR, and an antenna on top of it. In front of the television on the floor were a couple of movies that were not stacked neatly. Straight ahead kind of in the middle of the floor was a black wood-burning stove sitting on a piece of metal next to pails of paper, wood, and coal. A sage green office-like leather chair that had wheels on it was straight ahead with a table in between the floral designed couch and the chair.

On the other side of the couch was a huge collection of newspapers; some were so old the color began to change due to the smoke from the stove. He kept those for the fire to heat the house. I can remember how everything was placed, without much organization, like it was yesterday. It smelled like soot from the stove that was not very pleasant to the nostrils. My brothers and I always wanted to put the coal in the stove to heat the house. It was amazing to us to watch the coal, wood, and paper burn up in a matter of minutes.

Straight ahead was a bedroom with two dressers and a big bed, with a window and closet. This bedroom was in the center of the house almost like it should have been a hallway because there were no doors. Directly behind the master bedroom was another room with one dresser and a bed that was up against the wall, where there was a window to the kitchen with a curtain. Next to that room was a bathroom small enough for one person, a sink right in front of the door, a toilet that was very close to the sink, and a tub with no shower. The bathroom was so tiny that you could put one hand on the tub, the other on the sink and put a foot on the toilet without straining.

Every Friday he was faithful about picking us up right after school. We could not wait to get out of the house and go to the country. Sometimes he would take us to visit some of his family, like his daughter and son. Before we left town, we would get movies, and some kind of snack, normally cinnamon rolls or donuts, which were his favorite because he didn't have any teeth. If we went to the movie store and they didn't have what we wanted to see, we would go and get movies from his grandson. Some of our favorite movies to watch during our visit were with Jean Claude Van

Damme, Arnold Schwarzenegger, Sylvester Stallone, anything that was action-packed. We watched every Rambo and Rocky movie that came out during our time there. We stayed up late at night watching movies without a bedtime. Uncle knew not to get any scary movies because we would wake up having nightmares.

Uncle never cooked for us; I don't think he knew how, so for dinner most of the time, we would have pot pies or frozen meals. For breakfast he always had milk that came in a red and white carton and Grape-Nuts cereal, which we hated, so we always said we were not hungry. He did like eating the fresh eggs that the chickens laid; I was not a fan of them either. When you opened the refrigerator, no matter what, there would be milk and fresh brown eggs inside. If we went out to eat, it was usually fast food, which was a privilege for us. Our mom could not afford for us to eat out that often, so a lot of times we persuaded him to take us out.

I enjoyed going there because he was always nice and attentive to me and he didn't discipline us that often. We were able to play in the yard, chase the chickens and walk back to the pasture and see the pigs and cows with no worries. Uncle would always buy me anything I wanted like clothes, bikes, snacks, and would even give me money because I had become his favorite. The first brand new bike that I ever got came from him. It was a red ten-speed. That was great because before we always had used bikes, and that was my first big girl bike. I was so excited to ride to the store, park, a friend's house, anywhere, just to get on my bike. The only bad thing about having the bike was that it was at our house and on the weekends, we went to Uncle's, and because he lived on a gravel road with no sidewalks, there wasn't any place to ride the bike, so we couldn't take our bikes out there. He did get us some cheap old bikes and we could only ride them around the house. We did try to ride the bike on the gravel road and each time, one of us would wreck, so we learned to only ride in the yard.

I can only remember one time in all the years we went to Uncle's house that he physically punished one of us. We had just gotten to his house and he had bought a dozen donuts. He didn't care how many we ate, but we had to make sure we ate whatever we took out. So there we were being greedy little kids, eating one right after another. Uncle got up to put some trash in the coal bucket and spotted at least one donut in there that my brother did not eat. This made Uncle very angry because he did not believe in wasting food at all, and before we knew it he took his belt off and whooped my brother. We were all in shock because he never whooped us, he barely told us no or to stop doing something. Needless to say, we never wasted anything else around him. We ate all of our food and drink from that point on.

My mother became comfortable with him and let us spend the night more often, and we were so excited. At first my brothers and I would fall asleep on the couch while watching movies. After a few months he made the boys sleep in the back room by the bathroom and I would sleep on the couch. As time progressed he became more affectionate with me, wanting me to sit on his lap, hugging me, and even rubbing my leg whenever he would shift gears in the truck. I really didn't pay it much attention because I was so young and most of the time he pretended it was an accident.

One night while I was sleep, he picked me up and put me in his bed, and I slept so well. The bed was really high and came almost to my shoulders and had five or six heavy blankets on it. Every night from that point on he would bring me in the bed with him and no one ever said that I shouldn't go, but I knew something was wrong with me sleeping with this old man. I was sure neither my brothers nor anyone else knew about it because they would have stopped him immediately. Sometimes he would wake me up and lead me to his room, but only after the boys were asleep. He came and got me in the middle of the night and put me in the bed with him. The covers were so heavy it felt great during the winter nights because sometimes the fire would get really low or go out altogether and it would be extremely cold in the room. Uncle would pull me close to him and make sure I was warm. Feeling like this was not how it was supposed to be, I tried to stay on the couch, but he still came and got me in the middle of the night.

One night when he came to get me, and he was naked. Evidently something happened to him to cause his private parts to not become fully erect and he had a colostomy bag where his urine drained into. This time when he put me in his bed he began to caress me in a very adult way. After that I would make sure I had on plenty of clothes to make it difficult for him to get to me. But soon he started taking my clothes off, so I soon was naked too. I tried to pretend to be asleep, but he would still touch me, and eventually he did things to me that a child should never be exposed to. Anything that adults did in the bedroom, he tried his best to do it with me, using every part of his body. I didn't understand why because his private did not work, so I wondered what was the point? But he still continued to try. I lay there feeling nasty while he was sweating and enjoying my underdeveloped body. I was so afraid, I didn't know what to do: scream, cry, or fight. I was numb from what was happening, and I vowed to never go back there again.

Please remember this happened while I was in the third grade going into the fourth. I really had no power or control, so the next weekend we had to go back again. Every Friday after school when it was time to go, everything about me, my attitude, and demeanor changed. Once there, I always tried to stay outside with the kids or do anything that took me away from him. Sometimes it would work during the day; however, nightfall eventually came.

The first time he kissed me with his mouth open, I was sitting in the green chair on his lap while my brothers were outside. He pulled me towards him with slight force and put his tongue inside my mouth to kiss me. I thought I was going to throw up, it made me so sick. The smell of his breath, urine from his leaking bag, and sometimes bad body odor were smells I can't easily forget. After many months of this happening, he began to lay me on the bed without any clothes on and take pictures of me with a Polaroid camera. I lay there feeling helpless and ashamed. He kept the pictures in a drawer in his dresser and sometimes even hung them on the dresser mirror while I was there. I begged him to throw the pictures away, so no one would see them, and I was hopeful he would listen, but he never did. He never threatened me, but I felt no one would ever believe me or I would be in trouble for allowing it to happen, so I never told anyone. Uncle took my pride, childhood, freedom, dignity, and innocence away and I have never been able to recover them. This was a part of my life I became used to and after about five years of the abuse, I thought it was normal.

The odd thing about all of this was I felt like he loved me, and I was his girlfriend. I would get jealous when he wasn't paying attention to me. My feelings were hurt when I saw him with another girl or woman. In my mind I thought that this was how things were supposed to be. He went to a woman's house for hours who lived about three blocks from where we lived, and I would ride my bike to see if he was there. When he was, I was heartbroken. Now I look back and wonder how in the world I could have possibly thought this man cared for me and my well-being, when he was actually putting me in harm's way. How could he love me when love is pure? How could he love me when he was hurting me? How could he love me when I didn't even know what love was, and he was making it hard for me to ever find the true meaning because of his perverted and selfish ways.

LABEL 3

Ugly

My mother became very close with one of her friends who moved into our home and it was not a peaceful time at all. When alcohol was in the mix, things became very violent. Many times in the middle of dinner something would be said or done and plates, food, cups, ashtrays and even the coffee table would turn into flying objects. As my brother and I tried our best to eat, we knew we could not say anything. During all of the commotion, I asked God to please make it stop. The police would show up and make one of them leave, never taking them to jail, then after the alcohol wore off they would come back together. Most of the time it was my mom's friend who would be the one to leave because my mom had us in the house.

The hardest part of having her in the house was that she could not stand my guts but loved both of my brothers. She never wanted to touch me even in passing; she would throw herself up against the wall, arms spread out to the side like she didn't want to touch me as if I had a disease. By any means necessary, I would avoid being close to her, so that I wouldn't have to be mistreated. Walking past her could lead to being tripped, being called a bad name, or given a dirty look. She made it very difficult for me to be happy; this was part of the reason going to the country became normal for me. At least Uncle wasn't mean, and he wanted me around.

Growing up we were very poor, but my mother always worked to provide the basics: food, clothes and shelter. My mother even used to work in the corn fields detasseling corn, going to work at about five in the morning and getting home well after seven in the evening many nights. My mother has always been a very hard worker, but sometimes we just didn't have enough. One day when my brother and I got home from school, I could see that my mother was not in a good mood. As she prepared dinner and it was time to eat, she put candles on the table and told us we were going to have a candlelight dinner. The real reason was because she did not have money to pay the electric bill, but she didn't want us to know. Many times I hear people say, "I didn't know I was poor." Well, I knew we were poor, my friends knew we were poor, and so did everyone else who knew my family. Struggling was a part of who we were, but even if my mother had to make up something for dinner we ate every night. It always seemed as if everybody in the neighborhood had new name brand clothes and shoes all the time. My brother and I had to wear things from the Goodwill, yard sales, and sometimes family, but Mom made it work.

We could not afford a new washer and dryer, so we had an antique washer with the wringer on it and when it was time to wash clothes and my mom's friend was home, I knew it was going to be a problem for me. I tried so hard to make sure she was happy and to do things perfect in her presence, but it never worked. Washing clothes literally took an entire day because we had an old washer and no dryer. The first step was to get the bucket, fill it up with water from the sink and carry it back and forth to the washer until it was full. Second, we had to put the clothes in the washer and wash them. Third, we placed the wet clothes in a bucket and carried them to the other end of our shotgun apartment. Fourth, we filled the bathtub full of water and rinsed the clothes out by hand, then put them back in the bucket. Next the clothes needed to be run through the ringer and hung out on the line in the summer, and in the winter put on the heating stove. Finally, depending on how dirty the water was, we had to empty the water out and do the process all over again.

One particular Saturday we didn't rinse a pair of jeans out good enough and soap was still on them. My mom's friend took the wet pair of jeans and threw them at my chest with all of their strength, knocking me off balance almost to the floor and made us rinse all of the clothes again. Things like that happened all the time and when my mom found out about it, it started an argument, but for some reason she never made her leave. My mother tried to take up for me, but it only caused a lot of confusion that probably wasn't worth the hassle.

My mom's friend always tried to get a job but could not keep it for whatever reason. She finally got certified to drive eighteen-wheeler trucks;

boy, was I happy about God letting her pass the tests and get that job. She absolutely loved driving the truck and so did I because it meant she was gone for weeks at a time, and that's when our house was normal and peaceful. My baby brother was her favorite, and it showed. His punishments were always lighter than mine, and she gave him money and gifts without me knowing. So when he knew she was on the way home, he was so happy because that meant more gifts. She brought all kinds of stuff from shirts, to storage boxes, and the best was when she gave us money. Yes, I did receive gifts as well, but my brother's gifts always seemed to be better and more. The things didn't make me happy, though, because I knew in my heart it was just for show. That was another example of me not fitting in and it was worse because it was in my own house. Still to this day, many years later, I don't understand why she did not like me. I believe she could see the anointing on my life even then, and the devil used her to try to stop me from my destiny early on.

When we were born God had already predestined us, and if the devil can label us early on, he thinks that will kill us and our purpose. None of the tactics he used on me worked, and I still smiled and went on and understood my life would not always be like that way. I knew one day I was going to be an adult who made sound choices for myself that were healthy and made me happy. Uncle always made me feel as though I was beautiful and wanted, but my mom's friend made me feel the complete opposite of what I was. The ugly label was put on with extra holding glue, that took extra ripping to get off.

LABEL 4

Defender of the Enemy

By the time I entered sixth grade we weren't spending as much time with Uncle, so that was when I began to heal mentally, physically, and emotionally. That was when the labels of ugliness and insecurity began to loosen. Those labels were not ripped off entirely; however, my confidence was on the rise. Sitting in class I received a note to go to the office where two ladies were waiting for me. Both of them began questioning me about the man that had been molesting me for years. I was so nervous and wondered how they found out because I never told anyone. They told me that he was molesting another girl and they either heard or thought he was doing the same to me because of the amount of time I had spent with him.

I knew the girl who had made those allegations and was shocked that she too had fallen prey to him and his sickening ways. I thought to myself, *Here is my chance to tell and I'll never have to have his grimy, old, wrinkled hands on me again.* My heart began to beat so fast, my hands became sweaty. I tried to utter the one word that would probably put him in prison, but the only thing I could say was no. Those two women kept asking over and over again in many different ways and my answer remained the same.

There was no way I could say that he had been touching me inappropriately and then have to deal with my mother and the shame of not saying anything sooner. Walking away from the meeting with those ladies and not telling the truth was the worst thing that could have ever happened. I have never forgiven myself for not telling the truth. I could have saved so many other girls from going through what I went through.

It was horrible not being able to sleep, being afraid, and feeling disgusting during and after he had his way with me.

I feel the reason he chose to touch another girl was because we had stopped going to his house. Every time my mother would ask if we wanted to go, I would tell her no, so eventually she stopped asking and I was happy. Now don't get me wrong, I still had contact with him because he would still come over to our house and I'd see him at my aunt's house. He seemed to be angry with me because I didn't want to be around him, but I was okay with that. He began to treat me very differently, barely speaking, stopped paying attention to me and even tried making me jealous. The fact that I wasn't made to go to his house made me happy. When the visits slowed down and finally ceased, so did all of the gifts and money. It was almost like I was a prostitute. He got to touch and feel on me, and I would get stuff. When he didn't get to touch and kiss me, there were no gifts. I was not even a teenager, yet I thought if I gave him what he wanted, I would get what I wanted and both of us would be happy.

LABEL 5

Sexual Abuse

My mom would always have company over and they would drink and sit around talking and reminiscing about the past. Her friends told us what my mother was like when she was young, and it made us laugh. She did have a set of friends, a couple, and they were at the house all the time. The wife was sweet, and I had known her many years. She was married to a man who was from another city and was extremely nice as well. When they were around, we would laugh and have a good time. They didn't have any children so many times they were at our house very late into the evening and ate dinner with our family. My brother and I liked having them over because that meant we could stay up past our bedtime. We didn't have a door to our room that was connected to the living room in our shotgun apartment, so sleeping with company over was really not an option.

The husband became very friendly and was always willing to help in any way. If the chain, tire, or anything on our bike messed up, he was always there to fix it. Once he got comfortable with our family, he began complimenting me on things such as my clothes, shoes, hair, anything that would get the attention of a developing teenager with low self-esteem and insecurities. There were many times when he would spend time with me and my brother talking and playing with us. My mother and his wife ran a quick errand once and he stayed at the house and watched us while we completed homework. I asked him for suggestions on what to write for my homework assignment, which was "If you had one place to go on a dream vacation, where would it be?" He responded with "the Virgin Islands" and he said that he would take me. That has always stuck with me, but it was just another example of him being inappropriate. When he passed me, he would get as close as he could and put his hands on my waist as if he were holding me.

When I think of him I think of a lion that watches its prey. It knows just when to attack. A lion doesn't growl and make noise, which would warn the prey to run away, but it sits back and watches and strategically plans the attack. He watched me for about a year until he started to learn my weaknesses and where I was most vulnerable. Once the lion figures out the plan, he knows that he will have dinner for the day. When the lion attacks he goes in full force, grabbing the prey with its teeth and dragging it around until it dies from its wounds. Once the prey has given up, the lion rips its lifeless body apart with its teeth.

The lion that was preying on me moved in slowly, making sure I could not get away. He became more physical with me when no one was looking or around, rubbing up against me like I was made for him. The desires that he had for me were not what an adult man should have for a twelve- or thirteen-year-old child. I tried to avoid him as often as possible, but it was very difficult with him being very close friends with my mother. He said things but physically he never tried to have intercourse with me, and although he encouraged me to touch his private area a couple of times, I couldn't. The only thing I could think about was here it goes again. What is wrong with me that only grown men are attracted to me? Why do they see me as being weak? What did I do or say to have these men prey on me? Could they see the labels from afar, or was I just that broken?

That really affected me even more because none of the boys my age liked me. My insecurities were already shattered due to my previous sexual abuse, sun-kissed skin, and a body that was too big for its frame. Feeling like I was not good enough even for myself, I was at my lowest. The sad thing is I couldn't tell my friends because they were related to him, I couldn't tell my mom because she was his friend, and if I told a teacher or someone at church, I was afraid I would be taken out of the only normal thing I knew and that was home. Most people would look and say that my home wasn't normal, but it was normal for me and it was what I knew.

Although I had already experienced so much in my life in such a short time, somehow, I found the strength to bear it in my inner self and go on in spite of the hurt. No one knew what I was dealing with, so I didn't have a cheerleader, a mentor, or friends who understood my pain.

I had to encourage myself. That season was very lonely for me and I felt misunderstood. I became very angry and began to act out at school, home, and church. I was mad at everyone: my mom, the "lion," Uncle, teachers, anyone who was in my space and face. I felt like someone would and could see that I was hurting and needed help. I was feeling like an infant who is unable to communicate with words but will instead scream and holler with tears flowing down their face, not just because of the pain but also the frustration of not being heard. Everything in me tried to say verbally what was going on, but due to my teenage immaturity, the words would not form and fall out of my mouth. When I acted out I was labeled as bad, and was disciplined but not loved, judged without a fair trial.

The seventh grade was a pretty decent year for me; things were starting to look up. The Speech team at school and church were ways for me to have some sense of pride in myself and accomplishment in my life. The Speech team was the one activity that I was able to control. I was able to control what category and topic I was going to perform. That was major for me because I never had any control over anything, not even my own body. The first piece I memorized and competed with was the "I Have a Dream" speech by Dr. Martin Luther King Jr. Every time I delivered his speech, whether it was for a competition, family, friends, or even church, I felt empowered. I found myself not being afraid of speaking in front of large groups. That really caught me by surprise, because how in the world could I speak out in front of crowds but not to one person who was taking advantage of me? That was part of the reason I chose that particular speech; I wanted to stand up for people who didn't have a voice, just as Dr. King did. I delivered his speech with authority and power and did it well with a lot of practice.

Church became my life. At church I actually felt the love and I felt that people truly cared. Wednesdays were particularly fun for me. The girls were assigned a teacher named Mrs. Diane. She really cared for us and made sure we were learning about Jesus. In her class we would design shirts with paint and glitter, eat, and have a great time while learning. She would take us to her house for sleepovers, swimming, and some type of craft. She really loved each one of her girls like we were her own children. One of the first major lessons she taught us she liked to call the love chapter from 1 Corinthians 13. It was hard for me to grasp the concept of love because the only love I knew was tainted, wicked, and was not normal.

Mrs. Diane somehow made us believe she loved us, not only through what she said, but what she did for us. I am sure I rejected her and acted like I did not want her close because when people got close to me it always ended up in disaster. She was excellent with us and always encouraged us to love without boundaries or restrictions as Christ loved us. Out of all the lessons she taught us, that was the scripture that I still remember from the first time we memorized it. She was able to break it down and give us examples that helped us understand. Love is an action word that is very difficult to understand without having a model to pattern after. The fact that I wanted love so badly probably played a major part in why I allowed the molestation to take place.

The older kids that were in high school had a different teacher and were able to do a lot more things due to their age. For example they went bowling, had bonfires, and took trips out of town. Although we loved our teacher and had fun with her, we could not wait to move to the next class. Sometimes we were allowed to go into the class with the older children and we loved being there with them. Even though we wanted to move on, there was something about the group of girls that were in the class with me. We were almost like sisters because we were together six days a week, including school and church. There were bonds formed there that could not be compared with anyone else's. I had friends that I was close to in my neighborhood, but it was different because we had shared personal stories. Even though I was close to those girls, I still didn't have the courage or confidence to tell them of my experiences.

During my eighth-grade year, my life became like a blockbuster movie that I starred in. I was the defenseless victim, and it was being directed by the "lion." It was almost as if he knew I would be good at playing the lead female role, so he gave me the role and I didn't have to audition. When he would see me at the park, store, or anywhere, he would say inappropriate things to me. Some of the things he said to me I was able to "deal" with, but when he began to become way too physical, he would rub up against me, hug me longer than necessary, kiss me on the neck, I knew it was not a good situation. I didn't understand why I couldn't just tell him to keep his hands off of me, especially already having rehearsed this scene just a year or two before. Even though I knew it wasn't right, still I liked it in an odd way. He made me the star and not a supporting actress. He was the only one in my life at that point who really made me feel pretty. My mother and the couple had mutual friends, so wherever we went with her they were there.

My mother had a friend who lived in an apartment complex a block away from us and we loved going to her house because she would let us stay up and eat all kinds of junk food. During one particular visit, the "lion" was there visiting another resident. As I was walking in the hallway I ran into him, and he expressed in a very vulgar way that he wanted to have sex with me. I couldn't believe that he was being so blunt. He had never been that outright bold before and I was perplexed. I told him no and added that he shouldn't say that to me, but due to the fact that he had been drinking, it went unheard. All I could do was think about what he said, how he looked, smelled, and grabbed me. I really wasn't afraid because I didn't believe he was bold enough to actually put his words into action. When I think about it, the prey of a lion knows the lion is going to attack; it's just a matter of when. How does the prey not know when they live, eat, and dwell in the same environment?

Later that night my brother and I were back at my mom's friend's house. We were having a great time playing games, watching movies, and eating snacks. Not having a bedtime, it became very late in the night and we were still up. I am sure all of the sugar and caffeine we had consumed also had something to do with us still being awake long after our bedtime. Finally when the last movie was over, we decided it was time to call it a night. I wanted to sleep on the couch, so I didn't have to share the bed with my brother. Now I wish I would have gone in the room because my life was about to be changed forever. My worst nightmare could not have prepared me for what took place next.

As I lay on the couch, for some reason I couldn't sleep and was wide awake. There was space between the door and the floor, so I could see the light from the hallway, which was kind of distracting to me. I laid there for what seemed like hours, but in reality, it was only about one or two hours. As I watched the light under the door, I saw a shadow that stopped at the door. My first thought was who in the world is up this late walking around in this building? The shadow never left from in front of the locked door that was there to protect me and the other people in the apartment. I became really afraid when I heard the door being tampered with, so I closed my eyes and began to pray, thinking we were about to be robbed.

The door opened and there he stood, the mean raging "lion," ready to attack. Still wondering how he was able to get in through a locked door, I knew this lion was ready to devour me and my childhood. I closed my eyes and pretended to be asleep, but that didn't matter to him. He came over to the couch after shutting the door to the bedroom, smelling with the stench of alcohol and smoke. He began to kiss me in my mouth, but I kept my mouth closed so he could not kiss me. I closed my eyes tightly, knowing what was about to happen. He pulled the covers back and pulled out his private. Keeping my hands clenched tightly so I would not have to touch him, I said "Stop, please don't do this to me, stop, stop, stop." He lifted up my shirt and pulled my panties down. At this point I was in complete panic mode, holding my legs tightly together to make it difficult for him to force himself inside of me.

As I lay there I struggled to keep myself from this angry "lion" while he tried to force my legs apart. The door opened, and his wife entered the apartment, screaming, yelling, and cussing while he was on top of me. She made her way to the couch and tried to fight me; he grabbed her to prevent an altercation. At that point everyone in the apartment was up due to the disturbances that were taking place in the living room. His wife called me all kinds of horrible names, such as slut, hoe, and nasty, to name a few. In the midst of the chaos I tried to pull my clothes back up while crying, shaking, and begging someone to call my mom. We only lived a block away, so it didn't take my mom long at all to get there. My mom came in and tried to figure out what was going on with literally five people screaming at one time. His wife kept calling me names, wanting to physically harm me, so my mom made sure that ceased quickly. My mother was so distraught she gathered my brother and I and left.

Everything seemed to go blank; I could not grasp what had just happened to me. Even though I had been through molestation before, this was totally different. Uncle was never violent, aggressive, or forceful. When we arrived at the hospital on an early Sunday morning to get a rape kit done, I became even more devastated. That was the most humiliating thing that I had ever had to experience. Everything about it was bad, even the doctor. Not knowing what to do, my mother called the youth pastor from the church, and he came and prayed with us and helped comfort me and my family. At the time I didn't think the "lion" had entered me, but when the kit was done at the hospital, the doctor said he saw it differently. He wasn't able to enter me fully because of the fight I gave him, but our private parts did make contact. The doctor was not nice at all; it was almost like he thought I wanted it to happen to me. Every label that was slowly being ripped off began to re-attach itself stronger than before.

When the police finally arrived at the hospital to take my statement, I told them exactly how it happened, including the comment he made to me in the hall. Here you have a thirteen-year-old child describing things in detail that were never allowed to be mentioned to complete strangers in any other situation. The one good thing was we lived in a small community and my mother knew the police officers, so there was ease with that. The officers could not believe that the abuser broke into the apartment to have his way with me. Although, I could tell they thought I let him in, they acted as if they believed me. Later, there was proof of the lock being tampered with. After the experience itself, the procedure at the hospital, and the statement with the police, I was emotionally, physically, mentally, and spiritually exhausted.

Finally after the day I had, my mother took us to get lunch and then medicine from the pharmacy. I tried to eat, but I wasn't able to because my nerves were so bad my stomach was upset. I tried to take the medicine that was prescribed for me, but as soon as I swallowed it, I vomited it back up. I tried to forget about what happened, but all I could see was the "lion's" face while he was on top of me. I tried to sleep, but every time I closed my eyes, the horrific scene from the movie of my life played over and over again as if it were set on automatic rewind. Have you ever felt like you tried so hard to fix something, but it never was enough? I gave all I had to erase that part of my life, but for some reason it wouldn't go away. It has faded but has not completely gone away.

The most disappointing thing about all of this is I told, I defended myself and the "lion" was never captured and put away like the animal he is. My life was changed forever because of him and he did not have one consequence for his actions. When I saw him around town I avoided him at all costs, no matter the setting. I was more afraid of him than of Uncle because he was young and very forceful. Uncle was old, and I knew he was no longer a threat to me because of his age. This person took another piece of me that will never be replaced nor recovered.

I was very angry with my mother because I felt as if she could have prevented some of the pain, disappointment, and abuse that I endured. Although my mother did not know what was going on pretty much in both cases, when does the "mother's intuition" kick in? The question is if she would have known, what would have been different? Would my childhood and innocence have still been snatched from me like a person struggling to take their last breath? I am not sure of the answer, but I do feel that because I was given to her from God and life is the most precious gift that anyone can receive; she would have done all she could to protect the thieves from robbing her only daughter of the happiness that she deserved.

LABEL 6

Unwanted

The summer following the incident I went to stay with my aunt in Cardinal until school started. I was so happy about going for many reasons, the main one was I didn't have to see the "lion" for at least two months, and I was getting out of the small town. My cousins were all older, so I hung out with them at the arcade, they would take me places with them and I got to ride the bus. My aunt moved out of the Tower Apartments and lived in apartments where there were children my age, both boys and girls. I was able to connect with one of the neighbors, a dark-skinned boy with a few siblings. He always wanted me to walk to the store and hang out with him. The time we spent together was really good and slowly we started to like each other. The more time we spent together, the more I began to like him, and it felt good to be liked back by someone who was okay to have like me, someone who was my age.

It was a nice hot, humid day out, so we decided to hang out in the hallway of my summer fling's apartment. He always hung out with his brother, so we were never really alone. That particular day we talked, held hands, and hugged and I, for the first time, got butterflies. The hug seemed to last for minutes, but I know it really was only a few seconds. That was a feeling I'd never felt before and wanted to feel it at all times. Both he and his brother were older than me, so the peer pressure was strong. They wanted me to kiss him, but being the shy, abused victim, I didn't want to. After about two or three hours, I finally gave in. I had no idea what I was doing, but I gave it my best. Closing my eyes, I leaned in while he was sitting on the step and before I knew it, I was having my first kiss. Feeling very mature and like I had done something amazing, all I could do was smile. I couldn't wait to get back home to tell all of my friends that I had my first kiss with someone who was cute, older, and lived in the city.

The rest of the summer was going great. I kissed him a couple more times, but never anything more than that. Towards the end of the visit, my mother phoned and wanted to speak to me. During our conversation she stated that my brother and I would be going to live with my second oldest aunt. When she first told me I was mad, hurt, and disappointed because I thought she didn't want us. She said she needed to get some things in order and it would be best if we stayed with Aunt Liz. It was not a bad thing to stay with her; in fact, we loved to go to her house. It was peaceful, fun, and the love was there. I just couldn't seem to get over the fact that my mom did not want us in the house with her at a very crucial point in our lives. I was entering high school, which is a time when any child is more curious and susceptible to peer pressure.

Getting back to Indiana with my aunt, I had an attitude, became disobedient, and got into trouble at school. My freshman year did not start off well at all: in-school suspension, regular suspension, and many trips to the principal's office were just a few ways I was punished for my behavior. My aunt was very much a disciplinarian. She did not play when it came down to acting right at school. Many times when I got in trouble and they called her while she was at work, I knew I was either going to get a whooping or grounded. Being unwanted walked up from out of nowhere and sat right beside neglect. This label even had the audacity to get comfortable and not go home for years, even after an eviction notice.

LABEL 7

Loser

Church was the only place I enjoyed and being on the Speech team was the other outlet that I again turned to. The Speech team was absolutely wonderful, and I was able to escape from my world. The first year on the Speech team in high school I was trying to feel my way and find a good prose or poetry piece that I could relate to. I tried a Maya Angelou prose selection, but I didn't win, and I didn't feel like it was accepted well by the judges of the competitions. Saturdays at competitions became tough and I knew that piece just didn't fit me, but I was determined to always do my best. Placements were few and far between for me that year, with a fifth and sixth place ribbon here and there and maybe a third place one time. I knew I was better than that but needed the right piece.

My sophomore year on the Speech team I knew I had to do something that would cause me to shine and bring home some blue ribbons. One day my coach called me into her classroom and wanted to know what I thought about a selection of poems by Paul Lawrence Dunbar. Opening the folder I was in shock. Every single word that was typed out was in dialect and I had no idea what it said; I couldn't even understand it. The coach could see the disappointment on my face, so she grabbed the folder and began to perform it right in front of me. My eyes lit up and a huge smile spread across my face. This Caucasian woman had just performed an early-nineteen-hundreds piece whose character was a strict black mother, and she did it like a pro. I knew at that moment these poems were prize-winning. Day in and day out I practiced, practiced, practiced until I perfected it.

The season for Speech team had started, and it was finally my chance to see the rewards for all of my hard work. I went to about three or four meets and began to get second and third place, and I was not happy with those results at all. About halfway through the season I just wanted to quit, but instead I went to the meet not feeling confident in myself or my poems. The upcoming meet was one of the most competitive of the season. Believe it or not a speech competition was like a sport. There were opponents you had to compete against that became your rivals. I was at the toughest competition and I knew I didn't have a chance to win. Each contestant had performed all of the required rounds and the entire team gathered together in the cafeteria awaiting the results. With many different categories being announced along with the winners, I became uninterested and impatient.

Sitting at the table talking to the other members about random things, I was not focused on the ceremony at all. Prose was called and someone from our team placed and we all cheered. Next, the announcer said it's time for the poetry winners and again I continued talking. The winners from sixth place all the way to second were called and I knew if they didn't call my name, then there was no way I got first place. "The first-place winner of the poetry contest goes to Ryda Percy from Oakpark High School." Still talking and not paying attention, he announced my name again and I started screaming and crying from the excitement. That was the first time I cried from being happy; every tear prior to that came from pain, misery, and sorrow. The nights and days of countless hours of practicing had paid off in a huge way. I was feeling very powerful, motivated, and accomplished. Finally, something that I was great at and able to successfully compete in. My esteem was being lifted slowly but surely, I loved me and my God-given talents.

Church was still very important to me. Anytime the doors were opened, I did everything in my power to go, never missing. Growing up, going to church regularly was always a part of my life, even though my mom and aunt never went with us. We wanted to go, so we did just that. When we got in trouble, we could not go anywhere or do anything but go to church. My aunt would strip us of everything, but never punished us by keeping us from the house of God. So if we were to get grounded, we could not wait until Sunday because we were going to be able to get out of the house and see all of our friends.

The church that we attended took pride in their youth program and made every effort to keep us involved. There was always something going on, whether it was pizza, games, trips, amusement parks, camping, some type of activity was planned regularly to keep our attention. While attending that church I experienced a few firsts, such as being in a hayloft, riding a roller coaster, and even canoeing. The very first time I had ever been in a canoe was with the youth group. Everyone in the group had to find a partner to share the boat with; well, since I had not planned to go because I did not know how to swim, I was forced to go with a novice. The long ride to the actual lake I was very nervous, and everyone kept reassuring me I would be fine, but I still was a nervous wreck because I couldn't swim. Our group finally arrived at the site and all I saw was a lot of people having a good time in swimming suits and innertubes.

Walking to get our boat with our life jackets on and listening to my partner say that she had done this before, she could swim, and she was not afraid, made me feel a little better. So we got in the boat with our lifejackets on and my partner said something like, "How do we use the paddles?" I knew then that was the dumbest thing I could have ever done in my life. Thinking that I was never going to see my family again because we were going to die. Someone from our group showed us how to row and steer, so we were able to move from one side to the other, but at least we were moving. We got the hang of it and were literally rolling down the river and I actually was enjoying myself. My partner and I laughed and made the best of it. She lost a shoe, we got turned around a few times, and even stopped paddling just to see where we would end up.

As we got close to the last mile, she decided to stand up, even though I told her not to. She was standing up moving around, pointing and talking all at the same time, which made me so uncomfortable. I was yelling at her, she was yelling at me and before I knew it, the boat tipped over. That would have been fun for someone who could swim and wasn't afraid. People from our group were getting out and swimming. I could not believe they would get in that brown, nasty, smelly water. There we were, boat turned over and no one to help us and neither one of us knew how to turn it back over. We were standing up in the water and every negative emotion that a person could have I had because if she would have just sat down, we would not have been in that situation.

We waited for help to come from anywhere or anyone. After about fifteen minutes of being stranded in the water with a boat that was tipped over, our youth pastor arrived. We both began to rejoice because we knew he would help us. He came over to the boat laughing at us and our novice mistake, but I saw absolutely nothing funny at all. The youth pastor got the boat right side up and wanted to make sure we were safely back in before he left. He told me to step in the boat with one foot at a time and I made sure I followed his instructions carefully. The next thing I knew I was under the boat and in the water, screaming for help. Either he told me the wrong instructions, or I did not hear him correctly.

There I was under the boat yelling, crying and screaming with an attitude. My youth pastor and my partner were cracking up laughing and that just made me madder. In the midst of laughing and my panic, he yelled, "Stand up, stand up." When I came to my senses I realized the water was only to my knees, and I had on a life jacket. As I stood up with tears running down my face, I just kept saying, "You made me drown." Shortly after my "drowning" incident, we reached dry land and I was one happy individual. Needless to say, that was my first and last canoeing trip to this day.

Sunday night youth groups were the absolute best. The youth pastor who was over us had many fun and creative ideas that made church exciting. I became very close to the youth pastor and he was familiar with me because my older brother was previously a part of the group as well. All of the kids in the youth group were able to call him at any time of the day or night to talk to him about our problems. He was very attentive and genuine when we needed a shoulder to lean on or a listening ear. There were many times things went on at school or an extracurricular activity and he would show up to support us. Many of the youth looked to him as a father-figure, even though he did not have any children of his own.

Most of our youth group felt as if he supported us and genuinely loved us for who we were. One program that we participated in was True Love Waits. That program was designed for youth who wanted to save themselves for their future spouse, children, and God. The main goal was to practice abstinence. That was a task for me because I considered myself as unclean and not a virgin, because of the things that had happened to me in the past. The youth pastor talked to us about how important our bodies were and told us we were a temple for God. Once I finally forgave myself, I really felt free.

True Love Waits allowed my peers and me to learn to love ourselves. Love was something that I never felt, and it definitely was not true. Love to me was sacrificing your happiness for someone else to be happy. How could I feel love when I felt like the sacrifice? So when I looked at that program I truly understood that True Love Will Wait. The participants in the program made a vow and were given a promise ring that was a reminder to stay pure. Anytime I felt like I was going to fall into temptation with a guy at any level, I would look down at the ring to realize I was worth the wait. Many times I wanted to give in just to feel loved, but I knew in my heart that sex did not equal love. For me it meant someone at least wanted to be bothered with me.

LABEL 8

Low Self-Esteem

God always looked out for me because boys never really liked me. In my four years of high school I only had one boyfriend and when I thought I was in love, he broke up with me. Again, my self-esteem took a bungee jump from what seemed like the Empire State Building. Why couldn't someone love me? What was so wrong with me that everyone kept leaving my life? He and I were never intimate, but we did spend a lot of time together and began to share secrets and feelings that I felt before but never with someone my own age. That was new to me but felt good, until the moment he rejected me. I sat in my room and began to fall into a state of mind that was very unhealthy and dangerous. Never thinking that I would be able to get over him, I pretty much fell apart, until one day I realized that I made it before he came into my life, so I could make it after he left.

So now you ask, how did God protect me? He protected me from people who would love me and leave me. He protected me from giving myself to someone who only wanted to see me stripped of my dignity and pride. He knew how broken I really was and knew I was not able to handle any more heartache and disappointment. At that time I was hurt, but now I understand why it happened that way.

When I was in high school I never made good grades. I became very angry and acted out because of the things that I could not control from my past. My mother always taught us that if someone hits you, "hit them back," and when I was in high school if a person looked at me the wrong way, I would hit them. I was what you would call a bully. No, I am not proud of it, but I have to be honest about who I was and who everyone else made me believe I was. People called me what I acted like and I responded.

Beating up people somehow made me feel powerful and my pain would disappear for the moment. The odd thing about me being the bully was that when the nerd, poor, or the unpopular student would get picked on, I would take up for them. Being sensitive to the least liked person was easy for me because I knew what it felt like. I never wanted anyone to be mistreated because of their status. Fighting to me was natural, my whole life I had to fight. Growing up fighting people who were close to my family became the norm. I really didn't enjoy fighting, but it was all I'd witnessed and known. Please don't get this confused, it was not just a physical fight but an emotional, spiritual, and mental one as well.

High school was where I realized I would either drown or survive. By the time I was in the twelfth grade, I was molested two times repeatedly by two different men, felt neglected by both of my parents, experienced poverty, and had thoughts of suicide. I thought that my life was useless and that my GPS of life had stopped working and had been trying to reroute me for years. All of those things that I experienced were enough for me to give up on everyone and everything that was active in my life. The statement that made me believe in myself was spoken when a teacher told me I would never graduate from high school and I would be a statistic. Everyone knew I was an at-risk student, but to have a person who is supposed to educate, empower, and encourage say that to me was devastating. At the time I didn't know why it was said, but now I know it took that to motivate, encourage, and inspire me. People have always said things to or about me that were the complete opposite of how I viewed myself. I had to learn that no matter what people say, if you believe who you are and what you were created for, their words are voided out of your memory. Knowing that someone thought I would stay broke, busted, and disgusted made me do something different.

It was right after Christmas break and all of the "smart" kids were filling out financial aid papers, scholarships, and college applications and I was still trying to figure out what I was going to do. Staying in town was not an option, and neither was failure. I went to my guidance counselor's office and said, "I want to go to college." The look he gave me was pure shock because in his heart he knew I wasn't the college type. He gave me the financial aid papers and I took them home, so my aunt could fill them out, but she had no idea how to help me.

The next day I took the information to my counselor and said, "I need help, my aunt doesn't know how to do it." He assisted me with the process until it was complete, along with filling out some college applications. No one ever said that it cost money to submit applications, so there I was discouraged again. Since I was in the free lunch program, I was given two or three vouchers that would pay for college application fees. After applying for three schools and being denied by two, again my esteem took a hit. Finally after waiting a few weeks, I got an acceptance letter from the University of Liberal Arts. That had to be one of the best days of my life.

The day finally arrived, my graduation day, the day when I finally felt as though I had accomplished something. Waking up with the excitement of knowing that in just a few short months I would officially be an adult was very emotional for me. As we lined up in the hallway to get ready to take our seats, the thought flashed before my eyes and I began to cry. As I sat in that chair waiting, listening to all of the speeches and waiting for my name to be called, the tears just would not stop. It's an amazing feeling to get something that you never thought would happen. As I made my way to the stage, I stood there with both of my hands holding my face as tears just flowed. The only thing I remembered was hearing Ryda Isabella Percy, being called and everything stopped as I reached for my diploma with a smile. Then all of a sudden, the crowd went wild like I had just made the winning shot in the NBA championship game. That day was perfect with family, friends, food, and gifts. Even though my family is small, they came and supported and even celebrated me.

One of the things that kept my car fueled wasn't the support but the doubts, negative thoughts, and discouragement from other people. I've always been the type that if you say I can't, I will do everything in my power to prove to you I can. You only fail if you don't try; if you try and lose, you didn't fail you just learned valuable lessons that could help you get to the gas station to get refueled. During that time in my life, I "thought" I had failed in many things, but the reality is those were simply things I hadn't mastered yet.

That summer was filled with many fears, doubts, and concerns. Coming from a family where only one person had graduated from college was extremely stressful for me. That entire summer I wondered how in the world could I go to college, if so many of my family members tried and weren't successful? How could I do it? They were a lot smarter, motivated, and were supported more than I was. My entire life I wanted to get out of my aunt's and mother's houses, but when the time came, I just felt as though I wasn't ready. The entire summer I tried to focus on working and saving money, so I didn't become one of those poor struggling college students.

The summer of 1998 led me into pure adulthood, which was difficult. I worked for a summer youth program where I was blessed to work in an office with some amazing people. The summer youth program helped me pay for driver's training at the high school. My aunt did not have a car and never got her license, so after getting my permit, I became discouraged because I didn't have access to a car to take my driving test. Again, the people I worked with were extremely generous and let me drive their cars to practice in and to even get my license.

Trying to prepare your entire life to move out into the real world in a matter of two months and not having clear direction of where to go can be very intimidating. Please remember that even though I had no idea what I wanted to do or be, I understood that education was my one-way ticket out and the opportunity to destroy every statistic that I was labeled with. I was just a young black girl who grew up in poverty and never witnessed people who looked like me, with kinky hair, thick lips, and a pear shape, that were educated. College was not really my first choice, but it was my only option.

The summer went on and I had to start thinking about how I would survive in college financially. My aunt and mother were not in a position to take care of me. Again, the summer youth staff came to my rescue and taught me how to look for a job. I got on the phone and called the University to see if I could work on campus. That was when I was directed to the Diversity Center where Mrs. Smith, Mrs. Cook, and Mrs. Haynes managed a safe haven for students of color. At the time Ms. Cook was starting a new resource library and she needed someone to run it. When I went to the interview she explained that it would only be six hours a week at $5.15 an hour. I told her with a smile and excitement, "I will do it." Once the job was out of the way and I had my schedule, I was ready to get on the road to success.

As the summer finally came to an end, I was about to save about four or five hundred dollars after all of my necessities were purchased for school. Saving money was essential because $30.90 per week was not going to allow me to live and eat. So there I was at the end of the summer and I still hadn't worked out transportation to a school that was forty-five minutes away. Stress rose up within me because I didn't want to go through the entire process and not be able to arrive on my scheduled date. I had been in church my entire life but not saved, and I never really understood the importance of favor, grace, and mercy until I was fully mature spiritually. About a week before it was time for me to go, my neighbor asked me how I was getting to school, and my response was, "I don't know." Her response was, "Ok, just let me know when you have to be there, and I should be able to take you."

Low self-esteem existed much earlier in my life, but due to all of the other more powerful labels, it went unidentified until that point. When looking at me I don't think people saw low self-esteem. I learned to cover up my issues and just cope. Coping was not healthy for me, because it only covered up the issues but did not deal with the issues that taunted me and my future. I was broken into a million different pieces that super glue could not even hold together.

LABEL 9

Loneliness

God's favor landed right on me, and because I was too ignorant to understand the meaning of favor and blessings, I thought it was luck. People who believe in Jesus are not supposed to believe in luck. The bible in Jeremiah 29:11, [King James Version (KJV)] says, "For I know the plans I have for you," declares the Lord, "plans to prosper you, and not to harm you, plans to give you hope and a future." Nothing just happens, it's already predestined. Every trial, every triumph, your journey through the valley, and your rise to the mountaintop was in the plan of God. Nothing that you go through is a surprise to God. He created you and knows every situation you will face; even before your mother was created, Jesus knew you.

The day had finally come. All of my things were packed and put into my neighbor's van. Before leaving town, I had to stop by my aunt's job to say what seemed like my forever goodbyes. While I stood in the middle of her job, she gave me the "You are now on your own," speech. It consisted of "Do what's right," "Make good choices," "Go to class and do your homework." All of the things a parent is supposed to say when their child is leaving for college. Throughout high school I had a rough time with my curfew. For some reason every clock or watch I looked at was always an hour or two behind my aunt's. The final thing she said to me that memorable day was, "Don't stay out all night. Remember, the only thing open after twelve midnight is legs, and yours need to be closed." She handed me the watch from her arm and said, "Every time you come in too late and you look at this watch, you will think of me." Both of us busted out in laughter, but mine was accompanied with tears. Then we hugged, and I walked away.

On the ride to school, every single emotion one could have I experienced for the entire ride there. I laughed, cried, I was afraid, happy, excited, nervous, and feeling accomplished. The moment that I'd waited for had finally arrived, including getting the key to my apartment that was on campus. My neighbor dropped me off at the door, assisted me in taking my things in and then she had to leave to get back to her family. While standing in the middle of my room while this stranger (roommate) looked at me, it all seemed like a dream or a very interesting movie. After taking a few minutes to allow everything to sink in, I finally introduced myself to my roommate and struck up a very short conversation. The conversation seemed to be forced. She was very shy and introverted, and I was very loud and extroverted.

It was my first night away from home at a college apartment where no one and nothing looked familiar; I needed to find something to do. There were a couple of people I graduated with who I knew were also coming to the same college. The problem was I couldn't find them. Finally after walking the campus a little bit, I ran into my very good friend Ellis from high school. It was such a relief to see her. Once we got together we walked some more; there were so many people out doing the same thing. We met a second-year student and we went back to her apartment and began to talk. He gave us the ins and outs of college life from his perspective. Looking back on our first night, I now realize it was ignorant to allow this strange male in the house with us alone who we had just met and knew absolutely nothing about. That night was definitely memorable and the three of us hung out just about every day the entire first semester.

Monday came sooner than I wanted, but I knew I had to face my first day of college with a smile, determination, and motivation. As I approached my class, I began to feel a little more at ease because I knew that I had all freshman classes, and everyone was in the same boat as I was. Walking into the class made me truly think about how many people in my life, from teachers to family, had spoken against that very moment. Once the first class was over and I finally understood where all of my classes were, things got easier for me. My first month went by pretty quickly and successfully.

One day after class about a month or two into my college career, I became extremely homesick. Everything I tried to do to keep focused and fight through my loneliness did not work. I began to break down and weep. I just wanted to go home; it wasn't worth the pain. Crying uncontrollably, I called my Aunt Liz, and all I could get out was, "I just want to come home. I don't want to be here anymore." My aunt couldn't understand what I was saying and became frustrated with me because I couldn't stop crying. I could understand why she was frustrated. She thought something was wrong and somebody had done something to me. Once she finally understood why I was crying, she did show me a little compassion. She explained to me how important school was and reminded me of my goals, dreams, and she told me school was going to be the only way of accomplishing them. That talk with my aunt taught me so much and helped me throughout my college career.

The most valuable lesson from that call was no matter how hard things seem, you can't give up on yourself. By that point, I had already defeated the odds when I showed up to my first registered class. I had people who had given up on me, so I had to be the one person who knew I was more than capable of completing this journey for my future. Yes, I felt as though I was labeled at birth; however, I could never identify that I had been covered with labels. I had to learn to rip off labels that I didn't know were attached. Many people didn't think I would even graduate high school, let alone go to college. When my aunt reminded me of everything I wanted to accomplish, it gave me strength to make it a little further. That call did not mean that I would never miss home again or never shed any more tears, but what it did mean was I did not have to go back to living in low income housing, having no vehicle, or become a statistic.

LABEL 10

Heartbreak

The semester started to come to a close about the first week in December and I was sitting at the front desk in the Diversity building assuming the receptionist role. The door opened and in walked two males who I did not recognize as students. One of the males was short, chunky, dark-skinned, wore glasses, carried a briefcase and was not dressed in business attire. As he approached the desk, I was not attracted to him at all in any way until he opened his mouth to speak. All of a sudden it was like love at first word. I'm not sure if it was the briefcase or his voice, but whichever it was, I began to blush. He finally made it to the desk and I assisted him with the business he needed, then it was time to get down to the business of what he would be doing later. Somehow or another we exchanged phone numbers after exchanging names and basic information such as age, and where we were from.

My shift, which seemed to take forever, finally ended and I could not wait to call this twenty-three-year-old man who I was smitten with. Yes, I was flattered that he entertained my eighteen-year-old-immature self. After getting home I could not wait to call the number he had given me. I must have looked at it twenty or thirty times in a four-hour timeframe. Picking up the phone to dial Erick's number made my heart race at about fifty beats a minute and waiting for him to answer had my nerves on edge. After calling him two or three times, he answered, and the conversation lasted for almost five hours. Although I had one boyfriend in life, I never felt about him the way this one made me feel, without even touching me.

Just from our long conversation I knew that this was extremely special. Being stripped of my innocence at a young age, it was very important to me to abstain from having sex. Erick was so much older than me; however, he respected the fact that I wanted to save myself for marriage.

At that time I was dating someone else who was not serious, but he really liked me. When Erick and I got off the phone, I had butterflies, I could not sleep, and I was so excited to see and talk to him again. Erick agreed to come over the next day, but I had plans with the other guy and did not want to hurt his feelings. The plan was set. I would see Erick in the morning and then hang out with my other friend once he left. Yes, my plan worked, but the sad part is the entire time I was out, I only could think about the mature man and that was not fair. Everything that Erick would say brought on an adrenaline rush, and the way he looked at me instantly made me smile.

Eventually, I had to let somebody go and I knew in my heart it would not be Erick. I had to call the other guy and tell him that I didn't want to see him anymore. Of course he was blindsided because he truly cared about me and we had fun together. My goal was never to hurt anyone, but it is not fair to lead someone on, knowing that you do not have the same feelings they have for you. Yes, I felt bad when I had to tell him, but he took it better than I would have. One of the factors that helped me make this decision was I wasn't his family's favorite person. His family for some reason did not like me and to this day I still don't understand why.

Later that week after I ended the communication with the other guy, Erick took me on our first date. I was very nervous and like any other teenage girl, I didn't know what to wear. Finally I made all of those critical decisions every girl has to make when going on a first date, and Erick showed up at my door just like a real gentleman. He opened my door, made sure I was comfortable before pulling off, and even turned down the radio and entertained me through his amazing conversation. He began to focus the conversation on me, still trying to see what I liked and didn't like, things that made me smile, things that frustrated me, just wanting to know why he was drawn to me. Our first date consisted of dinner and a game of putt-putt golf with no expectations of being anybody but who we were. Once we arrived back at my place, he opened my car door, walked me to my apartment, kissed me on my forehead, and told me goodnight. That had to have been the best date ever and it came with no pressure at all.

Erick and I chose to move on with our relationship and became committed to each other. We became inseparable, and every day I fell more and more in love with him. When you are in love with someone, you should be able to say things that you love about that person. The first time he told me he loved me I believed him. When you grow up not knowing the way true love is supposed to feel, sound, and the way it should touch you, you tend to fall quick and hard when it's done in a way other than what you have known. It came to a point that every time we told each other those heart-pumping three words, I would say, "How much do you love me?" Erick was so creative he had something different every time, and I would have to put on my thinking cap, so he wouldn't outdo me. One particular time when the question was posed to him he said, "Have you ever been to a beach?" I said, "No." He came back with, "Have you ever seen sand?" "Of course," I stated with a flirty laugh, and a gigantic smile that was accompanied with butterflies. He said with confidence, power and strength from his heart that was made of flesh and was never hard, "I love you as much as the grains of sand that are on a beach. I can't reduce my love to a number." From that day on I never asked him again how much he loved me because when I wanted to, I would just add another grain of sand to the number. When days of doubt set in and the devil tried to make me think I was unlovable, I thought about a beach and saw all of the grains of sand that were there.

Coming from my childhood I never thought someone would simply love me because I was created, and my name was Ryda, but Erick did. He was different from any other man I had ever come in contact with. Erick listened to me, protected me, he cheered for me, tutored me, wiped my tears, laughed at me and with me, and most of all, he never judged me. It wasn't hard for me to offer all of the love that had been buried due to the abuse that I survived as a child. Erick and I had a bond that no one could even come close to breaking. When his family had a gathering, he took me and introduced me to uncles, cousins, siblings, and even his grandparents; this made me feel so wanted. The more I spent time with him, the more I wanted to give him everything because I felt as though he'd given me his all to make sure I was happy and safe. Once again the labels started to loosen up, especially the root of all my labels: rejection.

Abstinence was very important in my life and I knew that it was what God wanted me to do. Erick and I spent countless nights together and were never intimate, even though I wanted to be, but he encouraged me to hold out. Having the desire to give something to someone who you never willingly gave to anyone else to show them your appreciation was important. When I thought about how much he was there for me, and I could depend on him, it was such a relief to me.

Erick invited me over to spend the night and I wanted to, so I did. The longer I lay next to him the more my hormones raged. That night was different from the many other nights we shared. I just knew it was going to happen on that night and it did. I was very afraid and nervous after it happened, and I felt as though I'd let God down and I became angry with myself, but never with Erick. Believe it or not, I even tried to convince myself that I was still a virgin and we didn't go all the way. Erick knew I was very hurt and disappointed, so much so that he cried with me. Not one time even to this day do I regret giving myself to him first, only because he was very sweet and understanding. Having the experience that I have now with men, I just wish we had been married because even though I wanted to engage in this intimate act, God was disappointed in my sin. Out of all the experiences that I have had, the one thing I wish I could have changed was having sex before marriage.

Throughout the second semester of my college career, my relationship with Erick blossomed. We were together at least five days out of the week and doing things young couples enjoyed, such as eating out, dinner, movies, putt-putt golf, bowling and other fun things. We started going to his church and that's where I was introduced to paying tithes, which means ten percent of your total income should be paid in offering/tithes in church. Deuteronomy 14:22-26 (KJV) speaks in depth about how you should tithe and what you should tithe on. When Erick would give what looked to me like a large part of his hard-earned money in the offering, I have to admit I got an attitude. Erick would always pay for everything because he had a full-time job and I was the typical struggling college student. In my mind I thought paying that much in church would take away from our outings; however, that never seemed to happen. Sometimes it seemed as though we did more. He always told me, "This is something that God requires," and never minded what I thought or had to say.

One afternoon I decided it was time for him to meet some more people in my family. We arrived at my aunt's house only to find that Uncle was over there. This was very tough because Erick was extremely protective of me and knew what horrific experiences I'd had with Uncle. Erick stared at him out of anger through the entire visit, and when Uncle asked how I was doing, Erick responded, "She's doing fine, and she's well taken care of; I make sure of that." Erick was so angry about the fact that he was in my presence, I thought he was going to kill him if he looked at me just one more time.

That was when I knew Uncle could no longer hurt me in any way. I felt like the story of David and Goliath my entire life when I had to stand in the face of Uncle. Yes, I was David, the young weak teenager who everyone knew was not strong enough to win against the giant. Every time I was in Uncle's presence, the giant always won, only because I didn't know my strength. Erick helped me to face that giant with only a sling shot and five smooth stones. I knew that the next time I saw him, he would not try to say inappropriate things, because I was strong enough to fight back.

April came, and it was time for my birthday. I did not know what Erick was going to do, but I knew he would do something. My birthday is at the end of the month and I really just wanted to spend it with him, so all month I reminded him when my birthday was. He would always chuckle and say, "I know when your birthday is." On my big day I had to go to class and to work, so I was anticipating the excitement all day. The typical thing to do was dinner, a movie, and gifts, but not Erick … he knew I had never had a birthday party, so he wanted to surprise me with my first birthday party. When I came home and walked through the door, there sat Erick with some of my friends, decorations, a cake, and gifts. My emotions were so high, I could not believe he had coordinated an entire party on my behalf. He did things like that all the time to put a smile on my face, and he made sure he kept it there.

The semester was going well and so was my relationship. I could not have been happier. Erick was in management and one day after class we were spending time together and I knew something was a little off. He wanted to be strong and not worry me, but it was written all over his face that things were bothering him. When he felt comfortable enough he told me that he no longer had a job and would soon have to move across the country to the West Coast. I was completely devastated and could not believe that he was just going to get up and leave me behind. When I actually thought I was loveable and someone could pour into me in every way, it was just going to get packed, get on a plane, kiss me goodbye, wave, and leave. The feeling that I had, was something that I never felt before. My heart broke right there in that moment. Of course I began to cry and the only response I had for him was, "Why would you do this? I thought you loved me; I can't believe that you would do this to me." Erick claimed he loved me and had to get out of the city to start a new life. He promised we could still be together, no matter the distance. I was so hurt I could not hear what he promised, nor did I want to believe that he loved me.

Once I got over the initial shock, I was able to discuss this life-changing move with the one I knew God created just for me. We talked about when he would leave and all of the details that came with his departure. That conversation was filled with tears, laughter, and comfort for the both of us. The great thing about it was that he was leaving in the summer, so it gave us about two months to spend with each other and continue to water our growing love. Erick and I lived the last couple of months to the fullest. Not only did we enjoy each other, but we enjoyed his family. We visited so many people, I began to lose count of who we were visiting. Erick was never ashamed of me for any reason and was excited when I met members of his family. One of the reasons why I fell in love with him was because he loved and accepted me just the way I was. Every flaw that others preyed on, degraded, and pointed out, Erick embraced, cherished, and loved.

As the time drew near, it became more and more difficult to face the reality that he would not be around much longer, but I knew I had to find a way to overcome this heartbreak. There were many times when we would be on a date, and we stared at each other for long periods of time. Soon I would burst into tears. Looking at an airplane or even simple conversation with friends or family about traveling made me emotional. Erick could not believe that I was so messed up over him leaving.

The nightmare that I lived every day became a reality when I began to help Erick pack his belongings. He seemed to be excited about his new life, while I, on the other hand, was distraught, stressed, and overwhelmed. From the moment we began to pack, the tears also began to fall, and as much time as I had to prepare, it was still difficult. At one point I had to walk away from packing to cry. Erick was going to start a life for the both of us and it required him leaving what he knew and understood. That step in his life was necessary because he had to prove not only people wrong but himself wrong. Erick was born to conquer, he had no fear, and a determined spirit that would not be defeated by anything, especially the loss of a job.

The night before his move I did not sleep one minute. All I could do was watch him try to sleep. Erick would wake up periodically, and say, "Go to sleep, it's going to be alright." I tried to close my eyes, count sheep, pray, but nothing seemed to help me go to sleep. I laid there reminiscing about all of the special moments we'd shared, which only made things worse. I was up the entire night watching him rest because he was not worried about what was going to happen.

Midnight led to early morning and it was time to pack the car and start our journey of living apart across several states. Erick's mother and stepfather took us to the airport and that two-hour ride was the longest of my entire life. Of course his parents were trying to give him the advice only parents can give, and me being selfish, I wanted all of his attention. The more they talked the more emotional I became; I had to hold my head down because I didn't want his parents to see me cry. I was exhausted from not getting any sleep and wanted Erick to only focus on me. Yes, I do understand that at that moment I was being selfish; however, I felt like it was okay that one time.

We reached the airport and I told myself to get it together, so the goodbye could be memorable and pleasant. Erick and his stepfather got his bags out of the car and we walked through the airport to his terminal. Holding each other's hand with a firm grip, we arrived at his terminal. His plane wasn't leaving right away, so we had time to say our goodbyes without being rushed. The closer the time drew near for him to exit, the more I would fight back the tears. Erick told his parents goodbye and they allowed us to have our alone time while we said our goodbyes. During our time he reassured me that it would be a temporary separation and we would be together soon. He also focused on how much I meant to him and told me we were not breaking up. Erick and I embraced each other for what seemed like an eternity. He then put both of his hands on the sides of my face, pulled me close to him so our foreheads would touch, and told me how much he loved me. That was followed by a kiss on the forehead and a quick non-intimate kiss on the lips. Erick did get a little emotional and later told me he cried a lot, and that it was an all-around overwhelming experience for him.

When we got back to the car there was an awkward silence. Then as Erick's mother did many times, she gave me some motherly and womanly advice. She explained to me that I was still young, and I had my entire life ahead of me. She also told me how important my education was and at that point in my life I needed to focus on school. No, I didn't want to admit it, but she was right, I had to focus on my future. I would not be able to contribute anything to any relationship if I did not have an education and a good job. Erick did what he needed to do to better himself and our future and I had to do the same. Even though I was young, I knew the importance of marriage and that it should be the ultimate goal of any intimate relationship.

The weeks moved on and my second year of school was about to start. I was so excited because I had purchased tickets to see Erick for a week. Yes, I was the typical girl, shopping, laying out all of my cute clothes, and packing for the trip. Erick and I talked every day, a couple of times a day, about our plans for when I got in town. My plane was scheduled to leave on Monday and on Thursday the week before, Erick and I had an argument. It was very different and before I knew it we had broken up. I was in shock, so much so that I knew he was going to call back and make up. But it didn't happen. Because I was scheduled to leave the next week, I kept packing my things. I just knew he was going to call and say he was sorry. But that didn't happen either. The day that I was supposed to fly out, I had so much confidence that Erick would call and tell me to come, I didn't even cancel my ride. My ride showed up and was ready to put my things in the car and they knew something was a little off without me telling them. I explained to them that we broke up, but I knew he was going to call and I still wanted to go. I waited until the very last minute for Erick to call, but it didn't happen. That breakup was worse than him leaving because it was every bad dream coming to reality.

Trying to recover from that heartache was tough. I attempted everything I could think of to fill the void, pain, and disappointment I had but nothing worked. The pain was intolerable. The more I tried to mask my feelings, the deeper I fell into the pit of complete darkness. I was depressed; I could not think, work, function, or get out of bed. I was so in love with who we were together in just a few short months, I lost who I was without him. That was unhealthy for me, and the people around me even made comments about my appearance, attitude, and my lack of energy. What they didn't know was that I no longer had a life. I was a shell of a person walking around trying to just exist in the real world. The issue was I could not master just existing because I never really existed until I was with Erick and when he chose to leave, so did my identity. I could feel the labels squeezing the life out of my being.

Going back to school I knew I had to pull it together and rip off the labels of heartbreak. Growing up in church I understood that I had to find a church home and get rooted in Jesus. Someone told me that Jesus is the only one who can mend a heart that has been shattered by another person. One day I was talking to my beautician who had done my hair in high school and she invited me to her church that just happened to be in the city where I went to college. I decided to take her up on the invite and went to church one Sunday morning. She attended a Baptist church, which was what I had been a member of my entire life, so there were no problems with the beliefs.

Most people see me as a very outgoing individual who is the life of the party and will talk to anyone, but the reality is I am somewhat shy and meeting people sometimes makes me uncomfortable. Walking into the church I will admit it made me nervous, but I knew I needed to be healed and at that point in my life I needed an emergency room with a specialist who could heal me. I found my beautician and sat through the entire service with her and actually enjoyed myself and the people. After that initial visit I began to attend on a regular basis, eventually meeting more people, and getting involved. Church was just what I needed at that devastating time in my life.

LABEL 11

Sin

After attending church for a while and wanting to be involved, Deacon William Thomas, the youth pastor, invited me to help with the youth. That was so exciting for me, because the youth department was fairly large and on the rise. The youth pastor was young, creative, and full of energy and was dedicated to the lives of the children and the ministry. Deacon Thomas was a young man, which shocked me because every deacon I knew was old and, in most cases, mean. Not that deacon. He was only about eight or nine years older than the college students and was just getting into a career that he enjoyed, so he could relate to us. When I first started in the ministry I was just his assistant, but a very busy one. I assisted in giving children rides, blowing up balloons, preparing lessons, and any other task I was given. Being asked to do that was an honor and gave me worth. Those children were excited to come to church and to see the youth leaders, which gave me purpose to not just exist but to live and do what God created me to do. I began to reach for the labels and rip them off.

Over time, Deacon Thomas thought it would be a great idea to have the older kids separate from the younger kids. The middle school students heard the news and became excited as well. When I asked him who would teach that group, he simply said, "You," with a smile. That decision caught me completely off guard but made me so happy. It wasn't so much that I could not handle the responsibility, but the fact that Deacon Thomas believed in me. That was probably the first time in my life that someone actually believed in me, and it was even more special because he didn't know me that well. The connection that I had with Deacon Thomas grew because of the roles we played in the church. William lived only a few miles from the campus, so he would pick me and my friends up for every service, and never asked for gas money.

Having a church where I was able to work in the ministry and be fed was crucial for me. Deacon Thomas even created a group/fraternity for the high school and college age students as well. There were about fifteen or twenty of us in total, more college students than high school, so he went with a fraternity name. Our name was Theo's Pro'tos, and we took our group seriously. Just like a regular fraternity we had to be "initiated" in. There was no hazing, but we had special projects, assignments, and scripture verses we had to memorize, in order to take part. Deacon Thomas is a talented artist and he handcrafted notebooks for every member with a picture on the front that looked just like us. He did not just take a picture and decorate the notebook, he used construction paper and did it. Yes, the picture he created out of paper looked just like us. Everyone was excited when he surprised us with our notebooks.

At first we didn't know what the notebooks were for, but he explained the importance of taking notes from the lessons. In our notebook was where we put our assignments that would be graded weekly, our prayer requests, and questions. Yes, he took the time and graded our books, and if it wasn't right, he made us redo it. One thing he taught us was we had to have a complete understanding of the bible because when witnessing to non-believers, we needed to know our stuff. That was another reason why I really loved going to church. There were things created for our age group and a person who was totally dedicated to us.

Deacon Thomas went above and beyond the call of duty for every youth and young adult in the church. Many times in most churches the youth budget is the least funded, but he went into his own pocket and bought things that we needed. There were many times we thought he was getting paid and reimbursed only to discover he volunteered and donated his money. That was a sacrifice for him financially, I'm sure because he didn't make a lot of money, but again, he never complained. Even on a budget he made sure we had fun and were learning the word of God. Deacon Thomas was a firm believer in fellowshipping, hanging out, and being amongst each other. He planned outings with us like bowling, dinner, fireworks, and our favorite, the amusement park in Cardinal, Kentucky. Cardinal was so much fun. We got to sleep in the hotel, eat, go to the park, and see world renowned gospel recording artist Kirk Franklin. At first none of the college students were going to go because of our finances, but Deacon Thomas worked it out for all of the youth, young adults, and volunteers to go for free. No one had to pay anything. We were so excited and enjoyed everything about the trip. We talked about that trip for many months after. It was a blast.

Deacon Thomas would include us in everything, even when it came to purchasing his first home. He was in our age group, so we hung out often. One Sunday after church he told us he wanted to buy a house, so we spent many hours finding the perfect one for him. The journey was fun and exhausting, but we didn't mind because we liked looking with him and telling him what we liked and didn't like. When he finally found the house he loved, we all knew it. The house he chose was on the other side of town, a corner lot, with cute landscaping, an attached garage. It had two bedrooms, a study, and a fenced-in yard. Deacon Thomas named his house Sunflower, because it was yellow. Immediately after service he would say, "Who wants to go see my little flower?" The house was completely out of the way, but the gas and distance didn't matter. For about a month and a half we drove past his little sunflower at least once or twice a week. He was so excited, and we were excited like we were moving in; no one in the group become jealous or upset. We supported each other. William and some of us would attend choir concerts, sporting events, and anything we were involved in.

William became my go-to person if I had questions about life, church, family, or any other topic I wanted to discuss. One Sunday after church he invited me over to his mother's house for Sunday dinner. Yes, of course I went, I was a poor, struggling college student with minimum food and money. Ms. Thomas cooked the best food on Sundays and made sure I was full. These were the home-cooked dinners that college students longed for: fried chicken, greens, macaroni and cheese, cabbage, sweet potatoes, and anything else that a person could crave. From the first Sunday I went during my second year in college, I would go every single Sunday after that and even began to spend holidays with the Thomas's. Everything was made from scratch all the years I went for dinner. I never witnessed Ms. Thomas prepare anything from a box. It was amazing how she could create a cake that was delicious out of eggs, flour, sugar, and butter that were just sitting on the counter. Don't get me wrong, my mother and aunts could cook, but desserts were not their specialty. If I did not get a balanced meal any other day of the week I knew on Sundays I would eat a good meal.

Ms. Thomas was so sweet that she would feed anyone, no matter the size of the group. I would bring my friends to church and try to explain to Ms. Thomas that there were at least six or eight of us and we could go out to dinner instead. Ms. Thomas was not happy with that idea at all and invited all of us over for dinner. When we arrived there was a lot of doubt that we would walk away full. Matter of fact, we made plans to go out to dinner after we left Ms. Thomas's. God used her and the resources she had and stretched it to where she prepared for five and fed about ten, and we all had seconds. One thing that Ms. Thomas specialized in was making sure you were full. It reminded me of the miracle Jesus performed with the two fish and five loaves; he fed thousands of people with just a little food.

Not only was Ms. Thomas an excellent cook, but she could create anything a person could think of wearing with a sewing machine, needle, and thread. Many times I would give her a pair of pants that were too long, and she fixed them for my exact height. William once took her his sweatpants and he requested that the elastic be taken out of the legs, pockets added, and for her to take out the drawstring. The next week when we went to Sunday dinner, guess what? William had every request delivered to him and they were pressed and folded. Ms. Thomas became like a mother to me as well. We had very intimate and private conversations that I will cherish forever. She reminded me of my worth and told me things a mother would told her daughter about men. Although Ms. Thomas was divorced, she was one of the best single mothers I have ever encountered. Because of her experience with her ex-husband, who she spoke about openly, it helped me in future relationships.

Ms. Thomas had two other children who I laughed and shared memories with. Her daughter who is named after her and lived about three hours away, bought a house when she was in her twenties. I'd never seriously thought about buying a home until I witnessed her do it. Ms. Thomas and I would talk like mother and daughter, and I told her by the time I was thirty, I wanted to own a house too. I had no idea how that was going to happen, but I knew with God it could. Ms. Thomas is very positive and no matter how crazy your goal was, she would support it. She looked me in the face, never mocking or discouraging or laughing at me and said, "Well if Lydia can do it, you can too. She don't have a man either."

That was amazing to me because I never knew of any women, especially black women who were that young and bought a house while single. That was a goal that stayed with me in the back of my mind. Being about twenty-two at the time, still in college, and living on ramen noodles, I had no idea how it would happen. Looking back on that day, I learned that life and death are in your mouth; if you want it, say it. Even though I was going to church faithfully, the label of sin had attached itself to me. I knew that the sin was wrong, and I understood the power of God's word.

One of the many reasons that I admire Ms. Thomas is because she is truly a virtuous woman as Proverbs 31 describes in the Holy Bible. That scripture is very powerful and only a few women can fulfill it, even though many think they do. It talks about how the woman makes fine linen and sells it. Ms. Thomas as a single mother made her children's clothes, cut their hair, and even created games for them. That book also speaks about strength and honor being the clothing of a virtuous woman. Ms. Thomas has to be one of the strongest women I know, and she wears those garments so humbly. In the many years that I have known Ms. Thomas, she has defeated cancer three times, along with enduring major back surgery and not one time did she complain. I never understood where she got her strength from, so when I decided to ask her that, the response I got was, "God is good." She knew going through the events in her life the only explanation that she had was God. He had been everything she needed Him to be: a provider, healer, deliverer, and much more and she recognized Him for His greatness.

Being able to be part of a family like the Thomas's was an example of God's love. Not one time was I judged, segregated, or put out. I was able to see how a mother was able to love her children unconditionally. I was finally coming out of my valley of heartbreak and climbing the mountain of healing, self-love, and success.

LABEL 12

Defeat

School was going well, and my long-time roommate and I were getting along perfectly. She and I became friends and surpassed the title of roommates. I introduced her to my family, she hung out with my friends, and even though she was an atheist, she even went to church with me a couple of times. The only part of my life I wanted to be able to do better in was my math class. Math is nothing but the devil; I just didn't get along with it and rebuked it every class.

Algebra to me was like a foreign language that was created as a code for the secret service and only a couple of people understood the language. Throughout my college career I had some teachers who were really pulling for me and went out on a limb to make sure I would complete the course. One of my teachers allowed me to take my test home because I looked at the first test she gave me and ran out of the room in tears. Another teacher spent hours with me in her office trying to break it down to me, so I could understand. No matter who would help or explain it, I just couldn't get it. If I could be reimbursed for all of the failed or dropped math classes, my bank account would explode. God definitely showed me favor with the teachers because he knew I needed to pass.

One of the classes that I took was a sociology class in a forum with close to one hundred and fifty students in it. I'm not sure why, but all of the black students sat in the middle section at the back of the room. I attended a majority white university, so to look around and see people with the same complexion as you, in many cases was rare. Although all of the black students sat together, there was one girl who did not sit with us. I noticed her because of where she sat, and the fact that her entire demeanor was different. She was very quiet and shy but sweet. She was petite, barely weighing a hundred pounds, short, and light-skinned like the color of caramel candy.

The seat she chose was by the right entrance, directly by the door. I never liked to skip class, so every day I was there, and she would be there too, on time with little to say. I have been excluded so many times in my life, and I never want anyone else to feel that way, so I would speak to her every day and even invited her to sit with us. She would decline sweetly with a smile. You could not miss her, since she sat by the door, and I did not want her to think we were acting like we did not want her to be a part of our group. I tend to be obnoxious sometimes, and I did not want to keep pressuring her, so I eventually stopped asking her to join us.

One day when I entered she spoke to me first, which was completely out of character for her, so I spoke back. She went on to engage me in a conversation and asked me my name. I told her, and she told me her name was Tasha. From that point on we would hold mini conversations daily. Tasha was like a ghost; she was the first one out of class and was never seen on campus after that class.

During one of our conversations we discussed how the class was going and we shared our struggles about the class. We decided to become study buddies and help each other pass the class and the professor. I have to admit I was a teeny bit intimidated because when we studied, she already knew all of the answers. She was so smart. I felt as though she was a tutor, and not a study buddy. Tasha never made me feel dumb, she worked with me and made sure I was test ready. That made me realize why she sat on the front row with no distractions and refused to come sit with the group. Her education was important to her and she refused to be sidetracked just to fit in.

The more we studied, the more we talked and formed a friendship. Tasha and I were complete opposites: she was skinny, cute, light-skinned, quiet, shy, and definitely an introvert. I, on the other hand, was fluffy, loud, and not as easy on the eyes, chocolate, and an extreme extrovert. Because we were so different, I never thought that we would hang out and actually become friends, but God has a way of bringing people together.

Tasha was not involved in a lot of extracurricular activities, but I was. One of the reasons was because she worked close to full-time hours and was going to school full time as well. She was always busy and between work and school there weren't enough hours left in the day to have fun. Most of the time when things were going on around campus, I invited her and being who she was, she came. Sometimes I knew she was uncomfortable because of her personality, but she actually fit right in with everyone. People were drawn to her for many reasons, but one for sure: She was a great listener. Her major was social work and she knew how to help people and listen to their problems and offered solutions on how to fix them. In all of my young life I didn't know that young people could be so sweet. Tasha is also a very tolerant person; my own patience level is low. If I complained about something or someone, and she turned right around and found the good in the situation. Our relationship balanced out in that when she was way too passive, I added my aggressiveness and vice versa.

Have you ever had a moment in your life when everything lines up perfectly with your goals and dreams? Well during my third year in college, that was my reality. I mean everything was going great; I didn't have any complaints. My relationship with Tasha was growing by leaps and bounds. We shared secrets about our past, our relationships, our future, and even our strengths and weaknesses. Sometimes it's difficult to share your weaknesses with another person when you are not sure how they will take it and what they will do with it. Tasha was not like that. She put a lid on the confidential information I shared with her, so it could not get out. After meeting her mom, I could see where she gets her sweet, quiet spirit from. Ms. Young was a single parent who instilled the importance of education into Tasha and she listened to the advice her mother gave her. Ms. Young adopted me and took me under her wing as if I were her own child with no restrictions on her love. On some weekends Tasha would call and say, "Aye, we are going out of town; my mom and I want you to come." I packed my things and jumped in the car and sometimes didn't know the destination until we got to the hotel.

This is the label of defeat, but when God placed Tasha and her mother into my life I felt as though I got the victory. Surrounding yourself with people who love and care for you is a wonderful feeling.

LABEL 13

Cowardice

Tasha and I were out and about one day, and we stopped at a gas station. I probably wanted to get something to snack on, considering I was the thick one and was always hungry. When we pulled up, we were debating on what snacks to get and whether or not we both needed to go in. We decided that we both would go into the store. We walked around the store and purchased our things while being silly and talking. As we were heading out to leave from the back of the store where the drinks were in the refrigerated case, I thought I saw someone who looked familiar. I wasn't sure because they were in the back of the store and I didn't see their face. It really wasn't a big deal because I knew a lot of people in the city and I was only about forty-five minutes away from my hometown, so I saw people I knew all the time. I continued to talk to Tasha, not really looking to engage in conversation with anyone else, so I pretended that I didn't see anyone I may have known.

When we were close to the register to check out, we came around the chip rack and there stood the roaring "lion." He still had his back toward me, but I knew what he looked like because the image of him never left my mind. I knew his built, his smell, his voice and everything that made him the predator he was. I froze in complete shock, grabbing Tasha's petite frame as if she could protect me. I tried to hide behind her, but because she was literally half my size, that didn't work either. Out of the corner of my eye about fifteen or twenty feet away, I spotted a life-size poster that was standing up. Quickly I ran to the back of the store and hid behind the poster. By this time Tasha was freaking out because she didn't know what was going on and people in the store were looking at me strangely. The only thing I could think of was the "lion" trying to pounce on me, to incapacitate me so he could become full off of my innocence again. I had too much fear at that moment to be embarrassed or to try to explain anything.

We made it to the vehicle and I still could not say much and of course Tasha began to ask one million questions about my actions. While she was concerned, I could not talk about it yet, not because I didn't want her to know, but because I was ashamed. I could not believe I was not strong enough to stand up to him in my adult life and defend myself. He was much different than Uncle. For some insane reason, I always felt as though Uncle cared, and I knew he was too old to violate me anymore. Maybe it was because I'd spent time with him for years and the "lion" just crept up out of the brush, attacked me, and then devoured everything that made me normal. I started to weep right in the car and Tasha was still lost with no understanding, so she said, "It will be alright." Once she put her knowledge into action as a social worker in training, I opened up and told her what had happened. She knew of my past and what happened to me twice, but no details, no faces, and no raw emotions.

After the incident in the store with the "lion," I knew Tasha and I had gone to the next level in our friendship. I knew I could trust her, she had my back, supported me, helped me become the best I could be, would not allow me to fail, she loved me, and most important of all, we had a love for God. She was a true friend; the kind people wait a lifetime to meet and I was blessed with her early on. We were extreme opposites in everything and in every way, still we became close and in her I gained a best friend for a lifetime. People questioned me with a curious tone and said things like, "You mean you and quiet Tasha are best friends?" I responded with the biggest smile on my face, "Yes, why did you say it like that?" They responded with, "You all are just different, and it seems as though she don't talk at all." When ripping off labels, be mindful that in some cases we think we have a label ripped off, but it may seem as though we ripped another one. The way I felt that day in the store made me understand that the residue of labels can stick around for decades after the ripping.

LABEL 14

Laziness

My years in college were not filled with partying like most other students. I came to get my education and that was what I planned to do. Things were not always smooth, and many times they came with a struggle of some sort. I would try to eliminate the financial struggle by working. My mother instilled in us that we must work, work hard, and never think we were too good to do any job. I held on to that and worked as many as three jobs, while at the same time taking a full load of courses. I worked two on-campus jobs: Queen Burger, and doing some odd jobs, such as cleaning houses or babysitting. Jesus always took care of me my entire time in college and I never went hungry. There were times when I got down to one pack of ramen noodles and did not have anything else in the cabinets or refrigerator, but somehow the next day I would be full at the end of the day.

The roommate I started out with my freshman year was my roommate until she graduated four years later. She was one of the few people that I knew who graduated in four years. She worked really hard and took a lot of college classes, and came in with credits from high school. Her graduation was bittersweet. I was happy for her but sad to see her go. I didn't want to live with anyone else but her; for the last three years before she graduated, we lived by ourselves. We really were blessed because she had her own room and I had mine and we got along well. I knew she would graduate before me, but the reality of it didn't come until she packed her things and I was standing in the apartment by myself. Preparing for another roommate was kind of stressful, but nothing compared to what I had already overcome.

That summer before school started, I worked cleaning up the apartments that were on campus. Each crew would be assigned about three apartments per day to clean. It doesn't seem like much, but those students were just gross. The dirt and grime I discovered was unbelievable. It looked as if many of the apartments had not been cleaned the months of August through May. It was pretty bad. The moment I walked in, there was an odor so unbearable, it almost took my breath away. College students are some of the most unclean human beings that exist. The things we found, I'm pretty sure their parents would be disappointed. I really didn't mind it that much because I knew during the school year I wouldn't be able to work fulltime hours. Some of the people that worked there were not able to handle it, but I held on to what my mother told me. I also understood that it was just a temporary job and place in my life. It wasn't the best job, but it provided things that I needed, so I didn't have to go without. One perk that was offered to us was a bonus if we worked hard and had good attendance, so I showed up every day, so I could earn my bonus.

My fifth year of college snuck up on me and I had no idea when I would graduate. Math was a heavy, dark cloud that seemed to always hold me back and at the sight of sunshine, it dropped a foot of rain on my success. The first semester that year I wanted to finally conquer the first math class that I needed out of three. Attending class and getting outside help from tutors wasn't enough. I focused on math so much my other classes fell by the wayside. I chose to major in Interpersonal Communications and get a minor in Sociology. I needed one more class to complete my minor and had to drop it. I was flunking my sociology class because I didn't have time to study. That was very disappointing, but I'd rather have just one major and no minor, than be a five-year college drop out.

My major classes were not an issue for me because I loved speech and enjoyed being in front of people. The professor I had for about eighty-five percent of my major classes was so creative and made us think outside of the classroom. We were able to do service learning projects at the local after-school programs, community centers, and classrooms. Having to entertain elementary-aged children when you were not a teaching major had its moments. The places she chose were in the inner city, so that in itself was challenging. It was interesting to me that I was one of two black students, so when we went to do our projects, the kids loved us. We had to grasp their attention, so at any given time you would find us rolling around on the floor, rapping, and playing childhood games that brought back memories.

Our professor gave us the task to create a project we lived in our everyday life. We were put in groups with people who lived very different lives. It was exciting to see what the groups came up with. One group did a mock Grammys show that was held in a very nice room on campus. The group decorated the room, turned down the lights, and had all of the students who attended dress up. They created awards for the students in the class and gave out trophies. All of the students that were not in the group were sitting on the edge of their seats in anticipation, waiting for their names to be called. Our group had to present last, and we had concerns about how we were going to follow the Grammy show.

The group that I was in was very diverse, but I planned on introducing them to some culture. That was harder than I thought because the ideas were just not flowing for me. When our group met, we had no idea what to do the project on. Many ideas were brought up, but no one came up with anything unique, fun, and interesting. It was getting down to the last minute and we as a group had to make some decisions. I pondered what to do for weeks and nothing came to mind. I was frustrated. I took a poll on what people were good at: one student said she could sing, another could play the guitar, and of course, all of us had decent speaking skills. This was when the light bulb came on. I thought we could have a church service. Initially I was a little nervous about presenting that idea to the group because I didn't know their religious backgrounds or if they even believed in Jesus. Much to my surprise when I put it on the table at the meeting, the group loved the idea and was open to learn.

No one in my group attended church services regularly, and none of them had any experience in a black church. I knew it was going to be interesting helping them get an understanding since no one's schedule would allow us to attend a service on a Sunday morning. So I was left with doing the training myself. I had to teach them the order of service and how our church service went. We set up the choir, which included our whole group, we sang a very basic song. One member provided music by playing the guitar by ear, and he did well, considering he had no idea how the song really sounded. I believe Jesus blesses all of us with gifts and talents, but two gifts I know I don't have are singing and rhythm. Those two things did not make it into my genes, but I did the best I could. I taught them how to clap and rock in sync with everyone else in the choir. One of my friends heard about what I was doing and volunteered to direct us because she knew that doing it myself was not the best idea, and my professor was okay with it. The group invited their roommates and friends so that our service could be a success, and people came and enjoyed it. When I say we had an entire church service, I mean we did everything, and in the correct order. We prayed, had announcements, sang, took up an offering, and had a fifteen-minute sermon. That was the first time I was on a platform with an audience telling people about Jesus, and it felt amazing. The service came to an end and we as a group were happy, along with our visitors, classmates, and professor. We received a good grade, so our goal was accomplished.

LABEL 15

Racism

The professor I had for the class where we did the church service, made us think outside of the box and challenged us to learn in a unique way. It seemed like every assignment we did made us more and more uncomfortable, but we did learn from each one. The next assignment was probably my most favorite service-learning project we did in the class. When that project came up on the syllabus, I was mad, had an attitude and didn't want to do it, but once it was explained, I quickly grew to love it. We were tasked with interviewing a World War II veteran and reenacting the interview in front of the class. This stumped me because I was not from the area and knew I wanted to interview an African American vet. Almost everyone in the class found it difficult because at this time any living WWII vet was between eighty and eighty-five years old. Many of the vets from that war had passed away, were in nursing homes, or not in a good enough mental state to be interviewed. The process would be long, and I knew it was possible with hard work, but I had to be dedicated to the project.

My first step was finding a vet who not only was mentally, physically, and emotionally able to do the interview, but also someone who wanted to relive their experiences of that time in their life. I began to ask every person I knew: people at work, church, the stores, everywhere, and everybody. No one could assist me in this search for an African American, and I thought I would have to resort to interviewing a Caucasian vet. There was nothing wrong with that, but I really wanted to see the experience through the lenses of an African American during that time. After asking around for quite a while, one person directed me to the "Black" Veterans of Foreign Wars (VFW) Post. That was where I hit the jackpot. The man I spoke with told me he knew of one that may be interested. Well, guess what? All I needed was one. He told me he would reach out to him for me, so we exchanged contact information, and he said he would get back with me. When I left that meeting, I had the biggest smile on my face and called my professor to tell her that I may have found someone to interview. She was just as excited as I was that I could possibly interview someone I'd been hoping to find.

Waiting for the phone call was rough, but after a few days I did get the call I'd been waiting for. Not only did I get the call, but it came with good news too. The vet had agreed to do the interview and was excited about it and was happy that I sought him out, so he could tell his story. I was able to get Mr. Smith's contact information and call him to set up the interview. When I called him he didn't answer, and after three attempts, I kind of got discouraged. After one final attempt he answered the phone with a great attitude and eager to start the process. We were able to set a date and he invited me over to his home to do the interview. I was okay with that because I wanted him to feel comfortable. That was one project that I could not wait to do, but I had no idea of what to expect.

The morning of the interview I was excited and then the nervousness set in. Mr. Smith was older, so I had to make sure that I spoke loud enough for him to hear, slowly enough for him to understand, and ask questions that would not offend him. Yes, all of these things were a struggle for me because I tend to speak too loud, I talk fast, and I am not always tactful. Being nervous was just a natural reaction for me, especially having such a huge responsibility. Trying to figure out what to talk about and being concerned that he might not remember, since he was in his mid-eighties, added more pressure. The interview would require all of the communication skills I had been taught, as well as my listening skills. Sometimes it's difficult for me to concentrate, especially in an unfamiliar place with unfamiliar distractions. The entire day I kept going over my questions and making sure I was prepared to do the interview successfully.

As the day went by I knew the time was drawing near for the interview. The interview was scheduled towards the end of the day, so I had to attend class and work, and that did help calm my nerves. The neighborhood that Mr. Smith lived in was not in the greatest neighborhood, but I knew the area and felt safe. As I approached the residence, I came upon an old two-story, aged house with black shutters, overgrown landscape and rusted chairs on the porch. Prior to getting out of the vehicle, I said a quick prayer, took several deep breaths, and remembered to calm down and focus on the task at hand. Once I got to the top of the chipped concrete steps, I knocked on the door. No one answered. I continued to knock on the door three more times and a short, dark-skinned, bald headed, plump man with a faded blue-collared shirt, worn blue jeans, and suspenders came to the door.

The vet greeted me with a smile and a firm handshake. He invited me into his home that was dated, and unorganized. Mr. Smith led me into the kitchen, which was where the interview would take place. He offered me something to drink, then told me to give him a second. When he asked me to hold on, I thought he would get up and go to the bathroom or grab something to eat, but that was not the case. While still sitting at the table he began to unbutton his shirt and grabbed a kit off of the table and gave himself an insulin shot, right in front of me. I was taken aback a bit because it was unexpected, but it made me think he was comfortable, which was good. When Mr. Smith finished taking his medicine, he was ready to start the interview, and so was I. I got my pen, pad, and recorder ready to ask the questions I had prepared.

Mr. Smith was easygoing and excited to answer the questions I had selected. Personally, I am not a history person and did not know too much about World War II, but this was an opportunity for me to learn first-hand about a piece of history I had only read about in a book. As I asked him the questions, he was very detailed in his responses, and I could see the pride as he explained to me his experiences. Nothing about this interview was forced or uncomfortable, it was natural. His body language was very positive, he spoke clearly, proud, and strong with no sign of weakness or anger.

Halfway through the interview I could tell the questions had become more difficult for him to answer. I asked him about being black and fighting in the war, that's when his demeanor changed. He became angry, upset, and his tone changed because of the treatment he'd received before, during, and after his service to our country. Mr. Smith spoke about being placed in separate barracks from the whites, even while in another country, which was shocking to me because we were fighting for one cause. He told me that the white soldiers looked down on them and call them niggers even while in the midst of the war. Even though I could tell that bothered him, he stated he did not bow down to what they said, he was rebellious and fought back. Mr. Smith reminded me of Muhammad Ali; he did not want to fight in a war to defend a country that did not love, respect, or honor him as a man or citizen. This soldier was discombobulated and refused to be in another country fighting for the free land and still be treated as though he were a slave.

The story that stuck out the most to me was the one he told about when he came back home. When his assignment ended, he was happy to be back and felt a sense of pride even after the treatment he had received because of his skin color. Many would think that when he returned, the American people would have greeted him at least with a little respect, but to his surprise that did not happen. When Mr. Smith got on the plane, he was asked to go to the back; he did not put up any fuss and did it. After he reached the states, he said he had enough of the mistreatment. When Mr. Smith attempted to board the train, the conductor told him he would have to wait until the white passengers boarded and if there was room, he could then board. That was when the interview became real, transparent, and emotional, which was what I had wanted. When the soldier was told he had to wait, he became irate and called the white conductor a "honkey" and told him that he was getting on the train right then, and he would sit where he wanted because he had just come back from fighting in a war. He also told the conductor he would kick his behind right where he stood. He used many expletives to describe his emotions about that day.

That interview was life changing for me and helped me understand what it was like to be black during that time. I have been discriminated against many times before because my skin has melanin in it. The fact that someone sacrificed for an entire country and could not even be treated as an equal was disheartening. Mr. Smith had the same thoughts, which caused him, in my opinion, to become prejudice towards the Caucasian race. After the interview I had to reenact it for my predominately white class and white professor. When I reviewed the interview, I set up a meeting with my professor because I did not want to offend her or my classmates due to the harsh language that was used. My professor told me that I needed to deliver it the way it was presented to me, and it would not offend anyone. The smile on my face was so big, just knowing that I could give my classmates the other side of the story was exciting to me. Yes, my professor was correct, no one was offended, and the class even asked questions at the end of the presentation.

My classmates' reactions left me somewhat puzzled because most of them were from rural Indiana and were not used to being around black people. None of them acted as if it was a problem and I was completely raw when I presented my interview. My intentions were pure, I just wanted them to get a taste of what our everyday life is like even in this century. That interview made me realize no matter how great I am, I am still a black woman. No matter my sacrifices for others, in some people's eyes I will never be considered a hero because my tan is permanent. No matter how much I smile and pretend that I don't see the sales associate watching me from around the racks, I will never be noticed for my clean record. At the beginning and end of the day, people's perceptions will always be their truth. So, what is your perception of yourself? Your perception is all that matters, and it shouldn't be tainted by another person's view of you.

LABEL 16

Unworthiness

That class ended, and I felt good about my future. I had learned so much about myself. I was really proud, and my self-worth took another leap in a positive direction. That semester three students came to our campus and started teaching bible studies and were what I would call "super saved." Those three young men were very attractive, ambitious, and were on fire for Jesus. The girls loved them, but for the wrong reasons, so the bible studies would be standing room only with just a few male students. I didn't like going and only attended a couple of times because the females were going just to be seen and not to be saved, healed, or delivered. Yes, I was one of those females who turned into a middle school girl at the thought of one of those young men. Something was just different about these men that had all of us curious.

Fredrick was tall, dark, handsome, and he truly loved the Lord. I loved the fact that he was so sweet and had a sweet spirit. Most people that you meet are not sincere Christians. They speak about being one way and their lives say something else. Fredrick's words; however, matched his life and his works were just as he said they were. Those young men never cussed, went to parties, and always were caught being "good." That behavior is unusual for college students because that is the time in one's life when they can get completely wild, drunk, smoke, and forget everything their parents told them not to do. I was never a partier, drinker, or smoker, but I did engage in things that I now understand are displeasing to God.

In college everyone was broke, so many times people would cook and invite other students to eat. I would cook a meal and invite Fredrick over and every single time he came he would bring his two roommates, and I would be disappointed because I was trying to learn who he was. It was not that big of a deal because all of my roommates would be home as well, so we would never be alone. I finally asked him why he brought them. His response was, "Because you are single, and I am single, and we shouldn't be alone." My first thought was I am a grown woman and I know how to act in the presence of a man, I do not need a chaperone. I did not speak my thoughts aloud, I just responded with a fake smile and, "Oh ok, I understand." I lied straight to his face because I didn't understand, but because I liked him, I had to respect the fact that he even wanted to be in my presence.

After class one day I called Fredrick to see what he was doing, and he told me he was prepping for church. I asked if I could go with them and he said sure. Of course he came and picked up me and some other students on campus and we were off. Not one time did I ask what kind of church we were going to, I just went to enjoy Jesus. At that time I was very involved in my Baptist church and enjoyed going, but I wanted to see why Fredrick and his friends seemed so much happier, freer, and more disciplined than I was. Walking in the church, everything seemed to be the same, then a unified praise went up that I had never witnessed. Everyone in that sanctuary was clapping their hands, stomping their feet, and were using their mouths to give God glory. That was the first time I had experienced church to that degree and through my shock, I kind of enjoyed it.

When the pastor gave the benediction and we slowly went back to Fredrick's vehicle, I asked him what kind of church that was. He gave me a side grin and said, "It's an Apostolic church." I had never heard of it before, but I was open to hearing more. Fredrick went on to tell me that I must be baptized in Jesus' name and had to speak in tongues. Even though they were different and even the church seemed to be different, I wasn't really feeling it. As he continued explaining what it was to be Apostolic and the dress code, I knew I could never be a part of that religion. All of the women in the church wore long skirts, no makeup, or jewelry and I knew I could not wear a dress every day. I loved my jewelry, and every now and then I liked to wear make-up. To be Apostolic in my opinion, consisted of too many rules that would restrict me from having fun. That was the first time I was introduced to the Apostolic faith, and I was completely turned off.

Shortly after I went to church with Fredrick, our phones calls were shorter, the meals together ceased, and the way I felt about him disappeared. I was no longer attracted to someone who thought that I was going to hell because I didn't have the same beliefs as him. Everything about our friendship was altered by one visit to his church. We still spoke to each other in passing on campus, but there was nothing extra from either of us. I have always been a person to stick to my guns and I knew I was not about to change my entire religion after one visit to a church.

The bible talks about being unequally yoked and because he was saved, and I felt as though I was struggling and confused, I thought I was not worthy to be with him because we were on two different pages of the book. That may sound harsh, but it is the truth; experience will teach you what you wish you would have known in the moment. While I did not feel worthy to be with him, it did make me question my relationship with God. I wanted what Fredrick had, but I didn't see it necessary to change my religious beliefs. I wanted to still live my undisciplined life but have the peace that he had.

LABEL 17

Dumb

At the end of every semester you are required to meet with your advisor to schedule your classes. I had been going to class and not really keeping track of what I needed but knew to just keep chipping away at my classes, so I could graduate. That meeting was very different from the previously scheduled ones. I walked into my advisor's office, knowing she would give me a long list of classes that I still needed. When I entered her office, we talked and cut up because she was my professor for most of my major classes and we had formed a relationship. She looked out for me a couple of times when my money was low and allowed me to do yard work for her to earn money. One of the shocking things about her was that she was young, about in her late twenties, early thirties and was not that far removed from the financial hardship you sign up for in college.

As my professor began to look at the paperwork she had prepared, I asked, "How much longer?" She paused for a minute, and stated, "You only need twelve more credits." I said, "Are you sure about that?" Her response came with a reading lesson from her. She said, "Look right here. This is all you need." That was the best news I'd heard in five and a half years. I hugged her, screamed, cried, shouted and said, "Thank you, Jesus, thank you, Jesus." I have to admit, the entire time I was in college I doubted myself, so that moment was the true testament to what I could do. There was light at the end of the tunnel that had previously been filled with darkness and disbelief.

I understand that for each label in our lives there are milestones, lessons, and even a very dry desert. The labels come to help shape you into a person who is strong, courageous, powerful, and full of hope. No stage is the same, and no matter how bad or good the label is, learn the lesson. There are lessons to be learned every day. Many of the things I have been through are for me to share with someone else so that they can have the strength to rip off the labels. Even while in the desert, there is life of some form, and it's our responsibility as humans to find things to be grateful for. The lesson I learned while in college was endurance; no matter what comes your way, hold on and keep pushing.

When the start of the last semester of my college years arrived, I was numb, I really didn't know how to feel. The main reason I felt that way was because college had consumed my life and the fear of the unknown kicked in. For the most part everyone who began in the same semester and year as I did, had already graduated and they were already working in their fields. The reality of getting into a field I wanted, finding a place to live, and being completely independent was frightening. At that point I had to block all of the things that would make me lose focus and evict them out of my mind immediately.

There I was in January 2004, with just four months until I finished the biggest accomplishment of my life. In the back of my mind, I doubted my success, simply because my confidence was still handicapped by the previous experiences and failures I'd had. I had not put a plan in place that would help me get through the last semester. I began to totally put my faith in Jesus and trust Him enough to get me through the final stretch. My biggest concern was conquering the Algebra giant. I had to do that in order to graduate. The last math class I needed was the tallest mountain I had to climb during my time in school. I had already taken that class three or four other times and had either failed or dropped it. When you understand it is your last chance to succeed, you make it happen by any means necessary. You create a way to succeed, and you make the sacrifices to push yourself to your goal.

When your back is up against the wall, two things will happen: either you will fight, or you will flee. I have never been one to run, so I had to fight, and that's exactly what I did against the math class I needed. I formed my own plan of success and I made it work. No, it was not easy, but how do you invest five and a half years into something and then walk away a loser with the victory so close at hand? That semester I knew I had to get focused and not become easily distracted by everyday life, work, and family. I knew that in the end it would be worth every tear, struggle, and sacrifice to proudly say I graduated from the University of Liberal Arts.

Every morning at about 6:30 a.m. I would wake up and be the first one in tutoring when they opened up. Everyone knows that waking up that early for a traditional college student was practically unheard of, but in my case, it had to be done. There was a retired doctor who took the same math class I did and volunteered in the tutoring center. He was about five feet tall, stocky, gray hair that was balding in the middle, and he wore glasses and regularly carried a backpack. That tutor was probably the most patient man I had ever known. Every time he explained something to me I didn't understand, he would break it down to an elementary level. Most students who went to be tutored went in the afternoon in between classes. I went first thing in the morning and in between classes where many times I was the only one. My determination was never strong until it came down to that moment, but it was what I needed.

After a few days of doing the homework and going to tutoring, it was time to see if it was paying off. The professor stated that we would be having a quiz and I immediately began to get test anxiety. For every test or quiz I took during my entire college career, I would write the scripture Philippians 4:13 (KJV), which states, "I can do all things through Christ that strengthens me." If I was going to pass this quiz it would be because of Christ, so I got the quiz and began to work the problems. Everything on it looked as though it was a foreign language that I had never heard of. I laid my pencil down, prayed and recited my scripture. At that point the only thing I could do was have faith enough to believe that the outcome of me taking this quiz was going to be in my favor. I was nervous about the outcome, but I knew I had to put in the effort to be successful and all I wanted was a "C." When the teacher was passing out the graded quizzes, my heart was in pure panic mode, but then when he gave me my results, I just smiled. I could not believe that I got a "C" on anything that had to do with math, but I did, and I was so proud.

The semester continued, and things began to really come to light about my future. It was spring break and I did not have a plan for what I wanted to do, where I wanted to be, or anything. I went to Tennessee to visit for a couple of days and this was where things began to change. While on my visit, I met some very interesting people who I knew I wanted to stay in contact with once my visit was over. One individual I met I knew that I always wanted to think of him just after the first few minutes of meeting him. His name was Nicholas. I met him through a mutual friend and we instantly connected. When my visit was over, we exchanged numbers and we began to talk every single day, many times a day after I left. I did not know where things would lead, but I had confidence it wouldn't lead to a dead end.

Getting back to school to finish up my last semester, I knew it was going to be a breeze, especially since I had someone who was interested in making me smile. Although the conversation was good, and I enjoyed what I was hearing, I did not want this to be a distraction from graduation. I knew I still needed to pass this math class and I had to continue doing what I was doing to get a passing grade. Everything in my life was up in the air at this point. I knew May would be coming quickly and I still did not have a plan. The more Nicholas and I talked, the more we liked each other, and we decided to secure a relationship. He knew I would be graduating in about one and a half months and nothing was holding me in the city I was in. We talked about every option possible and what it would mean for the both of us. I did my best not to focus on the relationship, so I could just get across the stage; however, it became more and more difficult when I considered I could be homeless in a month.

With about a month left till graduation, I began to plan my own party. This was going to be the biggest accomplishment of my life and I knew I needed to celebrate it. Party planning was nowhere near my specialty, but I figured out everything that I wanted and made it happen. I booked a DJ, venue, got someone to decorate, and someone to cook. It was going to be the party of the year. I invited anyone who ever played a part in my life: family, old and new friends, teachers, and even professors. It was important to me that people who prayed for and supported me in the valley were there to celebrate me on the mountain. So in the midst of graduating, having a new long-distance relationship, and planning a party, I did not lose my sanity.

The middle of April quickly came upon me and I knew that it was time to crack down. The only class that had me concerned was the math class. In every other class I was in good standing with no issues. I knew that math would literally be the key to my future, so I continued to go to tutoring, ask questions, sit in the front, and do all of my homework. I continued to stay persistent in my efforts to pass that class, but how in the world was I going to remember every single thing that I learned in the last four and a half months for the final?

Again, worry began to set in, but I knew I had to give it my best. The math final just so happened to be the last final for my degree, so I had time to get extra studying in. I sat down at my desk, prayed, wrote my scripture, and jumped right in. I knew it was not the time to panic. Graduation was in two days. The test was timed like always. I took every second allotted and I was the very last one to hand in my test. When I handed it to the professor, I told him I needed a "D" to pass because I was moving to Tennessee in three days and could not take a summer course. Yes, I had decided to move to Tennessee and give love a chance again. The professor chuckled and stated that I would be fine and told me he had noticed all of my hard work. I left that class with the biggest smile on my face, knowing that the years, tears, and money that were invested would finally pay off. The dumb label was one that had attached itself to me even in the first grade, but after completing my last class, I ripped it off. If I could pass a college level math class, I was no longer dumb.

LABEL 18

Dependency

Saturday after finals came along with my new boyfriend and my family coming to town, and my party was officially underway. The same day of my celebration, my goddaughter was also celebrating her first birthday. My day was so filled with activities that I knew I was going to be worn out. My boyfriend was in town and chose to get some rest while I went to the birthday party because he knew it was going to be a busy day. The birthday party was a success, even though she slept through her entire party, the guests still had a great time.

Once the birthday party was over, I was able to go back and prep for my graduation party. I was so excited to be able to celebrate my biggest accomplishment. The reason it was so big was because I was only the second person in my family at the time to graduate from a four-year college. I was no longer the statistic that I was labeled by teachers and family, and this was the moment I would officially step into complete womanhood. I graduated when I was twenty-four, but I had never really been independent. I lived in campus housing, so I did not know what it was to pay bills other than phone, insurance, and cable. When you have been put out, never accepted in, and you still have the strength to cross a finish line that has been moved multiple times to make sure you don't finish, and you not only cross it, but you crush it, that was definitely a moment I knew needed to be publicly recognized. Planning it all alone was a pleasure because I was the one who knew the struggle behind the success and it meant more.

Family and friends began to call for directions, so I knew it was time for the party. Many invitations were sent out near and far, but I knew everyone would not make it. Of course I arrived at the venue late and a few family members had already showed up. When I walked in, I was blown away by how beautiful it was. I began to tear up almost like it was my wedding day. The decorations were beautiful: There were real flowers, candles, and color placed strategically throughout the space. When my decorator told me not to worry about anything and to focus on my finals, I did just that and allowed him to do his job. The food table looked amazing; Ms. Thomas came through and made fried chicken, green beans, macaroni and cheese along with a few more of her signature dishes that I had the pleasure of enjoying while in college. When she asked me what I wanted on the menu, I'm pretty sure I said something like, "Surprise me, you know what I like," and she did just that. The food and decorations seemed to be a bigger hit than my degree; my guests were happy.

My guests included all types of people: old, young, black, white, teachers, employers, classmates, friends, family, and church members. Ms. Diane even came and brought her mother, who was at least eighty years old. Her mother stayed on the dance floor all night and was the life of the party. I wanted everyone who ever knew me to come out and enjoy my accomplishment and me ripping off the dumb label. With the exception of just a couple of people, everyone I invited came. Everyone who was supposed to be there was and the ones who couldn't make it, sent plenty of love and gifts. One of my professors showed up and brought her mother and I was shocked she even thought enough of me to come, but she did. We danced, ate, talked, and fellowshipped with one another with smiles and laughter.

Throughout my life my relationship with my mother has been fairly rocky and all over the place. On the night of the party, I did not anticipate her coming, so I did not get my hopes up. Disappointment was something that I learned how to overcome while dealing with my mother, but that night she showed up. I was so happy, her appearance put the icing on the cake. Children, especially daughters, have a strong desire to have wholesome, happy, loving, and trusting relationships with their mothers, so her presence meant a lot. In high school I was not the best child or student, but one thing was for certain, my bad choices and behavior did not run over into my adult life. At that point in time in my life, I had never been locked up, I didn't have any children, and didn't use drugs or alcohol and I had just earned my bachelor's degree, so I was the ideal child. When she showed up to the party something happened that I never imagined would be possible.

As we were standing around the gift table towards the end of the celebration, and the guests were watching me open up gifts and cards, there sat my mother with a front row seat with the biggest smile on her face. I could see that she was happy, but throughout my entire life I had never heard my mother utter words that told me she was proud of anything I had done. That particular moment when everyone was celebrating me, she stepped out of the crowd, hugged me, and with tears in her eyes whispered in my ear that she was proud of me. Shock took over me and tears began to flow. That moment was like a mother seeing her infant child for the first time through a long and difficult labor. It's unexplainable, the feeling you get knowing your mother finally approves of something you've done. My mother coming out to support the biggest moment in my life and telling me that she was proud, was a moment that has been frozen in my mind. I remember that moment like it happened yesterday and nothing anyone else said to me mattered because my mother sealed the deal with her comment. That event was one I remember as one of the best times of my life. It's amazing how one comment from a person you've waited twenty-four years to hear say they are proud of you can have enough power to change your view of life.

It was about eight o'clock Sunday morning and graduation was just a few hours away. There was very little sleep going on the night before because I could not believe the one who people doubted had knocked every barrier out of the way, like Muhammad Ali did in the ring many times. Mr. Ali had the ability to make a knockout look effortless, all while trash talking and running circles around his opponent. I'm not sure how effortless I looked getting my degree, but to an outsider, it may have looked like I was a scholar. Many people did not know it took so many tears, sleepless nights, and much prayer for me to even start my college career, let alone walk across the stage. My graduation had hundreds of graduates who participated, so it was nothing like my high school graduation, which consisted of less than two hundred people. Graduation was held in a stadium where concerts and other major events were held, and it was packed. Emotions were running all over the place, tears were flying, and smiles were radiant.

Sitting there waiting for the speeches to be over and my name to be called must have taken one or two hours. Through the tears I gazed over the huge crowd to find my family and my cheering section, and there they were in the top corner, smiling and waving. Having my family in my corner was a sign that actions speak louder than words. Having my family attend caused the tears to soak my face as if I were in the midst of a water fight. While I was in college I got very little support financially, emotionally, or even spiritually from my family. My family never really had much to give, and we are not a mushy, emotional family that does a lot of hugging and saying I love you, so many times while in school I felt as though I was a ship tossed at sea with no sail. There were things that were just trial and error. Test it and if it works, keep doing it; if it doesn't, try something else.

Once the speakers spoke and the important people congratulated the graduates, the show started. As each student walked across the stage, my heart would fill with more joy. My turn was getting close. I stood in line smiling, numb to the fact that I was not a statistic, but a success. I had turned my barriers into steps and climbed my way to the top. When my name was the next to be called, I pushed my shoulders back slightly to poke my chest out with pride. As the president of the university said, "Ryda Isabella Percy," I walked across the stage as slowly as I could to enjoy the moment while smiling, and waving to all of my haters, supporters, believers, and strangers. The moment was surreal. I had planned that very moment out. I was going to jump up and down, scream, and dance across the stage, but I was too excited to do anything like that, so instead, I decided to act as though I had home training.

Graduation was finally over, and I walked around looking for my boyfriend and family. I never found my family because they left to get dinner and get back on the road to go home. My boyfriend had flowers and acted as though he'd been there through the whole six years of my journey, but in actuality, he'd only come within the last two months. Nicholas was very supportive of anything I wanted to do, so I knew that he would be around to assist in making me great. Nicholas and I stopped by the restaurant where my family was, and then went and had a quiet dinner with just the two of us. We reflected on the weekend and what was going to happen in the next few days and how we would execute my relocation from Indiana to Tennessee. The plan was already in place and I knew it would get a lot of negative feedback from my friends, since I had only known Nicholas a couple of months. My thinking was that I had nothing to lose, but everything to gain and I could always go back home if things didn't work out. The city I was in was not a permanent place for me because

I knew I would be restricted in my career choices, so leaving just made sense at the time.

My dream job was to work with at-risk youth, so I could show them a former at-risk youth who had made it and ripped off her labels. Most people don't want to be a failure, unproductive, or told that they will not make it, so they need examples of what it takes to be positive. In my younger days I had no idea I did not have to be disruptive and fight. I just did it because that was what I saw most.

In Sociology 101 I learned that you are a product of your environment, which means whatever environment you came from, you would inherit those traits, good or bad. However, I do not completely agree with that. You don't have to be a product of your environment once you are taught differently. When people are taught to do better, they become better, and then go back to the environment and teach someone else to be better. There is a root to the negative behavior and I want to assist these children in finding their greatness and digging up the root to the issues. Being rejected is often the root that stems from low self-esteem and lack of discipline; however, this label can be ripped off.

While still in Indiana, I applied for jobs and had a couple of phone interviews. One interviewer in particular liked me so well, I had a scheduled interview the week I arrived in Tennessee. The confidence I had from it was immeasurable; I just knew I had the job. It was working with at-risk youth, and what better person for the position than me? Things were looking up and the excitement was setting in, along with the nerves.

The morning after graduation, Nicholas and I packed up a trailer with all of my belongings and drove to Tennessee. I said my goodbyes and never looked back. People still can't believe that the only people I knew there were Nicholas and his daughter, but it's the truth. One thing I learned while in school is that God has put everything in me to succeed. The problem wasn't that I was not equipped, but I needed to remember to dig deep down and pull out the strength I needed in hard times. Yes, it was going to be difficult, but after all I had gone through already, all I needed to do was be still and float.

Every summer when we were young, my brothers and I attended summer camp and we took a swimming course to see where we were and how far we could go in the lake. Let's just say swimming was not and still isn't my strong suit, so I never fully learned how to swim. The first thing that we were taught when we got in the water was how to float, and that anyone can float. You have to be still and just lie there like you are in a bed. Don't move and you will float. During my relocation, I remembered that if I would just be still and float, I would not drown. I told myself, don't fight the current, just be still and float.

While driving to Tennessee I prayed and asked God to be with me and have my back. Making the decision to move in with him and changing my norm was absolutely insane, but I wanted to try. We needed to talk about the bills and what I would be responsible for, especially since I only had about fifteen hundred dollars in the bank and no job. Nicholas was old school and told me that I was only responsible for my car insurance and cell phone bill, which was only about a hundred dollars a month. My responsibility was nothing and I knew I needed to contribute in other ways, so I bought household items, gas for the car, food, and tried to pay for dates. My job interview happened the first week there and I just knew I had the job and would be able to help Nicholas with more of the bills; however, I was rejected due to my lack of experience. That was my first letdown from the move, but like every other time in my life, I bounced back. At that point I looked for a job every day but still nothing came through for me. Now I can honestly admit I slacked off after a month of no callbacks or interviews. My account was still decent, so I really didn't *have* to work, I just knew I *needed* to.

After being unemployed for a month, I knew that something had to give. I wasn't used to not doing anything. Through the entire process Nicholas was very supportive and encouraged me and told me to wait for the job I wanted, but I became impatient, so he helped me out. His family owned a couple of businesses and he made a phone call to get me a job at his aunt's daycare. In the beginning I was just happy to be working, and I was good with kids. I knew I wouldn't stay at that job because I was only being paid minimum wage and I was part time, which was about thirty-five to thirty-nine hours a week. When I got my room assignment, I could have fainted right there in the middle of that daycare. She had put me in the infant room. I barely knew how to change a diaper and couldn't even make a bottle. Motherly instincts were not part of the curriculum in college, and not having any children didn't make it any better. The babies cried for no reason even after being fed, changed, and rocked; they not only cried but screamed. My nerves were shot every day when I left work, but because I needed a job I endured. One day I was left in the room with eight screaming, unhappy babies and I broke down right with them. Sitting in the middle of the floor I cried while whispering a prayer, asking God to make a way of escape. After six months of that, along with other major issues, I put in my two weeks' notice, and walked away.

A week later I applied at Treasures to do the remodeling of a store. When I say I absolutely hated that job, I mean that with every fiber of my being. The management staff had no respect for us, we worked hard, and it was third shift. I knew immediately that would not be long-term. Minimum wage was $5.15 but we were getting paid $7.25 and for two weeks' worth of pay, I was bringing home about four hundred dollars. I was a college graduate and knew I was worth more than I was earning. My friends were making about thirty thousand a year, which averages out to about $15 per hour. Every night when I made the thirty-minute drive to work, I cried all the way, and also in the parking lot for five minutes before clocking in. We all knew that Treasures was only going to keep a few of us after the remodeling was done. Slowly but surely people were quitting and getting notices that their last day would be at the end of the shift. The day for my assignment to end could not come fast enough, so when I got my letter I was happy. People couldn't believe that I was unemployed and happy. On top of working third shift, I also started working at Queen Burger part time while at Treasures. When my assignment ended at Treasures, I just picked up more hours at Queen Burger.

One day after my shift at Queen Burger, I sat down and started looking over the last nine months of my life and knew I was unhappy. I called my Aunt LaLa because I was completely discouraged about working at Queen Burger, especially with a college degree and she said, "When you go to pay your bills they don't care where the money comes from, just do it until you can find something else." That short conversation with her reminded me that I can float through anything, I just had to make sure not to drown. While laying and floating in the water I was praying that some of the labels would soak off.

My relationship with Nicholas started to go downhill. His daughter and I had formed a love/hate relationship, and I was miserable in every aspect of my life. Church seemed to be a thing of my former life and didn't really exist anymore. I was tired of being tired and cried out to the Lord in the middle of our living room one afternoon. When I moved in with Nicholas, I didn't feel bad or convicted, but the longer I stayed, the more God pricked my heart. My prayer that day was, "Lord, if you get me a job where I am able to pay my own bills, I promise I will get out of this man's house and get back in church." Living in sin may seem fun for a while, but a person with a heart for God will become unhappy and will need to change the situation. Loving Nicholas became difficult because it was not the way God intended, and I did not want him to have to choose between me and his daughter.

Once again, I was job searching heavily. I did not want to lie to God; I wanted to keep my promise to Him. The bible says faith without works is dead, so I put some work with my faith and updated my resume, put in applications, and started interviewing again. After about a month I got an interview for a job about forty-five minutes away, working with welfare recipients. The excitement set in, but I didn't want to overthink it due to my previous letdowns. Driving to the interview I reminded God of the promise that I made Him, and I knew I would have to uphold my end of the deal. Walking in the door, I prayed a short prayer and allowed God to do what he wanted to do. The two people who interviewed me were very intimidating and I couldn't read them well at all. When I left I knew that I didn't get that job, either. I told Nicholas how it went, and he said it didn't seem as bad I thought. He was always very encouraging and made sure that I was taken care of just like a woman wanted, needed, and deserved. I waited for the call and just when I was marking it off of my list, the phone rang, and my future boss was on the other line. Holding back the screams was tough, but as soon as he told me my next step and I said thank you, I hung that phone up and screamed and jumped all over the room.

The first person I called was Nicholas, then Queen Burger, to give notice that I was leaving. The call came on a Monday and because I am a woman of my word, I made sure I looked for a place to live. My future boss wanted my first day to be on Wednesday, which came quickly. The excitement to finally be earning a salary and not clocking in was overwhelming but satisfying. This was my opportunity to make real money, live beyond what I was living and do it independently.

My first day I naturally was nervous, but that was overshadowed by excitement. The night before my first day I did not sleep at all and could not wait until it was time to go to work. I drove the forty-five minutes to the job and even arrived early, so I sat in the parking lot for about thirty minutes until start time. When I walked in the building, I was directed to the person who I was supposed to see, and she gave me a tour and introduced me to the staff. When the tour was complete, she stated that the other person who did what I would be doing was not there and she wanted me to meet her. Sitting at my desk in my cubicle, the only thing I could do was smile and the tears began to flow. Reflecting on my past and where I was supposed to be and being in the place God created for me, which was thousands of miles away from my past, gave me a spirit of thankfulness right there at my new desk. The tears came with joy because I was finally in a good place in my life.

LABEL 19

Judging

A few hours later just after lunch, the office manager came to my desk to introduce me to my "partner." My back was facing them as they stepped into my cubicle and as I turned around to greet them, I knew it was not going to be good. The first thing I saw was a floor length skirt that covered the shoes of the lady, a long-sleeved shirt, and a very plain woman with a very pretty smile. From the moment I laid eyes on her, I knew she was an Apostolic, judgmental, holier-than-thou church lady and I wanted nothing to do with her. We were introduced, and I wanted to scream. I wondered how this was going to work out if we had to work side-by-side. She reached for my hand and said, "Hello, I'm Zakeya Owens. Nice to meet you." Surprisingly she was very different from how I thought she would be, but I still had my opinion of her based on what I learned Apostolics believe. The rest of the afternoon we talked about everything from family, work, and even where we grew up. She told me she had two beautiful princesses, Uriah and Unik and an amazing husband named Zephaniah. That conversation taught me that she was a family woman who put her husband and her children before anyone else and there was no compromising.

That afternoon once I got home, I told Nicholas all about my day like I was a little kid who had just completed their first day of school. The topic of conversation was Zakeya and her religion. He didn't understand why I did not like Apostolic people and I began to share the history of my experience with them. My experiences were so bad that I did not even want to associate myself with anyone who believed that way. Too many times I was told that I was not meeting the standard that God set, and I was not going to heaven. There was never really any explanation of why they felt that way, they just pretty much said that I was going to hell. No Christian ever wants to hear those words, especially when you are doing everything you were taught. Nicholas understood why and simply said, "You don't have to believe the way she does, you don't have to wear skirts every day, nor do you have to go to church with her. All you have to do is work together and at the end of the day, go your separate ways." He was so right, so I kept that in the forefront of my mind.

My second day on the job, Zakeya and I spent it together as she trained me, and it was good. She is very detail-oriented, and I felt as though she did a good job of training me. After our morning training, we decided to run out and grab some lunch. We tried to figure out where to go and once we reached the parking lot, I looked over at my vehicle and saw it had a flat on the back passenger side. Instantly I panicked because I did not know anyone who could change my tire. Zakeya said that her husband could do it, but I did not want to bother him because he worked third shift and was asleep. Nicholas worked forty-five minutes away and was not able to assist in changing my tire. Zakeya saw that I was upset and wanted to help, even though she did not know me well at all, and I appreciated that. We went on and enjoyed our lunch and she assured me that it would not be a problem for her husband to change my tire, so after much resistance I agreed. It has always been an issue for me to accept help from people because I don't want to be indebted to anyone, but this was one time I had to do it.

The devil wanted me to go back on my promise to move out once I got the job, but I refused. Nicholas and I got the newspaper and an advertising booklet that had things people were selling and giving away, along with rental properties. There was a house listed for three-hundred-sixty-five dollars a month; I called to set up an appointment to see it. Once we reached the city and pulled into the neighborhood that seemed pretty decent, I didn't know what to expect. When we saw the house on the dead end of a short street, I thought, *This is the cutest, smallest house ever.* It was very tiny with hardly any storage room, but it had two bedrooms. I'm not quite sure of the exact size, but it had to be about four or five hundred square feet; enough space just for me.

Deciding whether or not to sign the lease for the house was an easy decision for me. The owner took us back to their house and I signed the lease with a sense of pride. This was the first time I would be responsible for "real" bills and that made me just a tad bit nervous. I remembered the promise I'd made to the Lord and He held up His end of the bargain, so I had to hold up my end and move out of Nicholas's house. This was the best thing that could have happened because our relationship was getting worse and worse every day. My main concern was how I was going to transition to another new town that I wasn't familiar with. After signing the lease, the search was on for furniture and other household items that makes a house a home. Even though our relationship was on bad terms, Nicholas assisted me with the move in a huge way. The only thing I had was a bed that my mother gave me and a dresser that Nicholas bought for me when I first moved to Tennessee. I needed everything and knew I didn't have enough money, but one thing my mom and aunt did instill in me was to be humble and never think you are too good to start from the bottom. We began looking at for sale ads and going to yard sales to find furniture and appliances. Our search was successful. I found a loveseat that let out into a couch for twenty dollars, a chair with no legs for five dollars, and end tables for about three dollars. The things I got were not in the best condition, but they were paid for and they belonged to me.

Once everything was purchased and the lease was signed, I began moving in the next weekend. Nicholas borrowed his father's truck and loaded up all of my things and I was officially moved in. I stood in my very own residence with my name on the lease and I was responsible for the upkeep and bills. There are no words to describe how I was feeling. My very first place was not an apartment, trailer, or low-income housing, this was the moment I knew I was coming up. My past was just that, the past. I was walking into my future and was able to forget about the past and move forward. Although I was twenty-five years old, this move was what sealed my adulthood. It would be the first time in my life that I was responsible and no one else had the key to the next door to my future.

Living at home until college with many roommates, then moving in with Nicholas, I had never experienced living by myself. Nicholas knew me well enough to know that I was afraid, so we worked out a schedule of when he would stay with me and vice versa. On Wednesdays Nicholas would come and stay with me after he got off of work and on the weekends, when he did not have his daughter, he would also come and stay over at my house. It worked really well for us because it left me staying by myself only on Mondays, Tuesdays, and Thursdays, which was less than half the week. I have to admit the first three weeks, I did not stay at my house at all.

I stayed with Nicholas and was ok with it. Nicholas was ok with it but did not see the point in me paying rent and other bills and not staying there, so he convinced me to stay at my new place. Yes, I was afraid, so every night I would leave the light on over the stove and in the bathroom, which lit up the entire house. After about a week or so of living on my own and with Nicholas coming to visit, things got more comfortable for me and I felt safe. Feeling safe is one of my first priorities and knowing that no one can hurt me goes a long way due to my past. I never want to be in a position where I voluntarily open the door to pain, hurt, or rejection.

Our schedule worked for us for a while, but I knew that Nicholas was not who God created for me. When people saw us together, they said we appeared to be the ideal couple and had everything together. My family liked him, his family liked me, we took trips together, had material things, but the truth was something was missing that a monetary deposit could not fulfill. For the most part I had stopped going to church and was just an every-so-often saint. We mainly went to church when Nicholas's mother would invite us. God was not the center of anything we were doing, and it showed in our relationship, hearts, and the way we treated each other. Being with someone and not having peace at night and constantly arguing over minute things that could be easily resolved, is not worth the consequences it brings.

A couple of months later Nicholas and I had a huge fight that got completely out of hand and ultimately resulted in our breakup. I have always wanted to blame him for us not working out, but I take full responsibility because I knew that he was not who God had for me. Things did feel good; notice I said things felt *good but* not *right.* It was a tough breakup and with me being new to the area it was even more difficult. Nicholas was not ready to end the relationship, but I knew it was time to let go. I could not continue living a life that was miserable and had so much anger in it. There were some loose ends that needed to be tied up, such as getting belongings from each other's houses, exchanging keys, and getting my cell phone, that he bought me for my birthday, out of his name.

When Nicholas and I finally tied up all of the loose ends, I found myself going to church with Zakeya more. The hope, strength, peace, and love that I needed would only be found in Jesus. I was tired of fighting and tired of being tired of my situation, so I had to run to my first love and that was Jesus. At first I was so uncomfortable at that church; everyone looked very homely and wore skirts down to their ankles and I definitely did not fit.

Each time I was in the presence of the church people I was uncomfortable, and I did not understand why. My life was still full of sin. I was still having sex, gambling at the casino, and living a sinful life. The pastor of the church was preaching hard truth that was convicting me, still, at that time I did not believe what they believed. It was hard to think that everything I thought I was doing right and pleasing to God, was stinking in His nostrils. When you have been raised to believe a certain way, then to even think that after twenty-four years it was wrong, was upsetting.

When I questioned something that the pastor said, I always asked Zakeya. One thing I quickly learned is that she is a walking bible. It seemed as though she knew all of the scriptures from Genesis to Revelation, what page number, paragraph, and even the exact verse and book. She had been saved for a long time and spent many days studying and being taught the word. This was beneficial to me because she never put her personal feelings into any of our conversations. When I didn't believe, she would simply point me straight to the bible. Everything in me wanted to not like her and turn my nose up at her very presence, but the more I didn't want to like her, the more I did like her. Have you ever tried not to like someone, and that person loved you in spite of? Zakeya was just that person. People in the church would frown on me and stop talking to me because of my million questions and the opinions that I formed, but Zakeya never turned her back on me.

Throughout my time of going to church I could feel that I was changing. Something was making me want to leave my world of sin. It was different. I initially thought it was that I did not want to be left out again. One of the worst feelings in the world is to be the "odd one out" in a group of people. When I would get around the church people I felt that way; I was the only one with pants, jewelry, and color painted on my nails. They were strict in what they believed, everything about them looked plain but "saved." Coming from a place of big jewelry, tight fitting clothes, and other things that made me fit in, was comfortable at the time.

Zakeya always tried to mentor me and reminded me of the things that were Godly, but until I wanted it for myself, I fought against it. For the most part, Zakeya's family became my family and that was the time I learned the meaning of "birds of a feather flock together." Most people see this as a bad thing, but it's not always bad if you hang around people who share your same interests. If you enjoy shopping, more than likely you will hang around people who like to shop as well. If you enjoy traveling and nice restaurants, that is what your circle will consist of. I really enjoyed going to church and building a stronger relationship with Jesus, so those were the people I started to associate myself with.

Zakeya and her family became my family, especially since I had no family in Tennessee. She and her husband invited me into their home and her daughters welcomed me as their own. Initially I was shocked that in this day and age a family would open up not only their home, to a stranger but also their hearts. I quickly learned that family truly lived a Godly life, not only in public but also behind closed doors. There were many times that the opportunity was there for her to act unseemly, but it always seemed as though there was a small voice in her head that would ask the infamous question, "What would Jesus do?" Her actions were to always do the right thing, even if it was questioned by the crowd. She is a true example of how we should love one another, regardless of flaws and shortcomings.

The way that Zakeya treated me I knew that what she believed and how she believed was real and actually worked. It was something that made me second guess my relationship with God. I wondered how I could go to heaven living the life I was living. Yes, I went to church, but I also was gambling, cussing, fornicating, and doing whatever else that was not pleasing to God. I knew there was something more for me, but I didn't want to stop doing my dirt. I wanted to continue enjoying my life and still go to church. Well, going to church was not enough, there had to be a lifestyle change and a commitment.

LABEL 20

Anti-Holiness

At some point in a person's life they get tired of being tired of a situation, and that is where I was at that time. I still had my reservations about the Apostolic beliefs, I wasn't sure if they were for me. The more I attended, the more questions I asked, even the pastor. This was a serious life change for me, so I set up a meeting with the pastor and his wife. I was a nervous wreck, but they made me feel comfortable and allowed me to ask any questions that I wanted answers to. One thing that was important to me was that we not allow the meeting to turn into a heated debate where both sides felt as though only they were right. They listened to me with care and understanding, and things went really well. One of the most important things that was said to me that night amongst the tears and confusion came from the pastor's wife. She told me not to worry about anything, but to just enjoy Jesus. When she made that statement, I took her advice and that was where all of my labels began to rip off and my life changed forever.

The following Sunday during service when all of the saints were clapping their hands, stomping their feet, running and shouting with a praise, I sat and watched. While sitting there I remembered what I was told in our meeting. Even though I wasn't sure exactly what enjoying Jesus meant, I did understand that it looked like everyone was enjoying Jesus but me. Growing up, I never really gave God the praise, so it was uncomfortable for me to do it. The lady who I sat next to on the pew grabbed me by my hand and said, "Praise the Lord, sister, clap your hands, tell God thank you." I was perplexed and was fairly clueless on what to do. I decided I needed to join in and enjoy Jesus with them. When my hands were clapping it was very soft and quiet, and my pew partner said, "Go ahead. Thank Him for your hands, your feet, breath, a job, shelter, food, just thank Him for everything." Something about that motivation made me realize that I owed God a praise, and I began to give God a praise like never before.

Church after that Sunday was never the same. The other saints had a pure, honest, and appreciative praise that God was well deserving of. I wanted what they had and prayed for God to give me a sincere praise and He did. An older church lady used to always say, "If you don't know how to praise Him just pick them up and put them down (feet)." Everyone else's praise looked as though it was strategically choreographed by a professional. I had no rhythm and I couldn't catch a beat if it slowed down and stopped in front of me. Before I knew it, I remembered that all I had to do was pick them up and put them down, and that's exactly what I did. Nothing was organized or on beat, but it was a praise from my heart and I know God accepted it.

That Sunday I felt as though I was standing uncomfortable and afraid before a judge, awaiting my sentence. When I began to praise the Lord, it seemed as though I'd just gotten off of probation. I was not completely free, but I felt the chains breaking. Although I was not totally free, the sounds of the chains breaking, and labels ripping sounded so good. I could literally hear and see the ripping of labels naturally and spiritually. There was something else I needed to get, so I could get off of death row and back into society. I heard a pastor say once, "There are only two times you praise the Lord: when you feel like it and when you don't." Every Sunday following, no matter how bad I felt or what was going on, I made it my business to praise the Lord with everything in me.

Although I was going to church and praising the Lord on a consistent basis, I was still doing things that were not pleasing to God. The good thing about being in church was that even though I was still willingly committing sin, I had a conscience. When I did something that was not "right" I felt bad. Going to church was doing me good and slowly I began to change and not do the things that I used to do and say. That was odd to me because I never really felt convicted before, and suddenly I was. The conviction made me want to do right because I didn't want for God to be ashamed or disappointed in me.

One of the first things I noticed that changed in my life was my cussing. Cussing was just natural and easy. I knew how to cuss and was good at it.

One day I prayed and asked God to help me stop cussing, and He did just that. Driving down the street on my way home from work, someone turned out in front of me and cut me off, almost causing me to have an accident. While being cut off I began to fuss and the first word that came out of my mouth was the "s" word. When I said it, it shocked me because I knew I hadn't cussed in a while; I was getting better, but I didn't realize it until someone cut me off in traffic. Prior to that day it was about four weeks, since I had last cussed.

The pastor preached about the Holy Ghost, but in a much different way than I was taught in my previous church. When I was growing up in church, a person that "caught" the Holy Ghost just shouted in a praise and that was it. In the Apostolic church the pastor talked about not *catching* the Holy Ghost but *getting* it. That confused me even more because I knew that before, when I caught it, it soon left because I was still sinning, and nothing changed. The pastor explained it, but it still was confusing, so Zakeya became my Apostolic interpreter. She always broke things down for me, so I could better understand them and willingly answered my questions, no matter how crazy they were. I truly appreciated her actions and concern. One thing that Zakeya always said to me, "You just need to be saved." I was offended by that comment until I understood what she meant. Most churches are focused on how many people attend, rather than how many souls will be saved.

Many pastors will compromise on the truth to pacify and grow the congregation. The pastor did not do that at the church where I attended. He gave us the truth no matter what. The saying "the truth hurts" is so true, and it did hurt me. Sometimes he would tell the truth so much till all I could do was put my head down in shame because I wanted to be better. I have always had a desire to do the things of God and to be who He created me to be. The pastor would say things like, "You can't live with your boyfriend and be saved," "Gambling is not what the saints do," "Walking around in defeat is not of God," and "God wants you to have the victory." Some of the things he said hurt because I was guilty of that very thing. Not only did he preach the truth, but it also came with a consequence, which was hell. The consequence really made me nervous, because I did not think I was that bad, but one thing I found to be true, the word (bible) will clean you up.

Going to church became my life and I was slowly but surely getting the lifestyle down. Just like the cussing, more unholy things began to just fall off from out of nowhere, including the labels. One of the best feelings in the world is the feeling of accomplishment. When you think there's no way you could ever give up something that you love to do, and then you just stop doing it, a sense of accomplishment sets in. I began to look closely at my current situation and it was stress free, drama free, and becoming sin free. For the first time in my life, I could truly feel the presence of God and what it meant to have an intimate relationship with him. Yet even in my transition to turning things around, something was still missing. The feeling was like building a brand-new house with large rooms, huge bathrooms, plenty of closet space, but the walls were white, and no appliances were included. Nothing on the inside was worth seeing; it was bland and not very appealing to visitors.

LABEL 21

Trust Issues

One thing that I have learned is you can't just call on the name of Jesus in the time of distress, when the storms rage, and peace won't be still. You have to learn to praise Him when things look good and when they don't. Getting to a point of totally depending on someone or something is a weakness. I know because I have been let down so many times in the past. Learning to completely trust someone and surrender your own thoughts and ways was harder than I thought. I knew that was something I was going to have to conquer sooner rather than later. The process was frustrating and demanding, but it would be worth it in the end.

When I finally got a job that came with a desk, business cards, and my own phone line, I was happy but still struggling financially. That was difficult because going to the doctor and paying all of the fees and costs, even with insurance, was not affordable. I never thought that the financial struggle would still exist even after going to college and earning a degree. The one thing that my professors never told me was that the real world is rough and no matter how much you spend on your education, you can still be financially unstable. I wanted to get a refund on my degree, when I had the feeling it was not worth it. That was especially true when I needed to go to the doctor and they wanted me to go to a specialist and I couldn't afford the deductible. That day I called my Aunt Liz, upset, and she encouraged me and told me if I needed to go that badly, then I should go and deal with the bill later. Aunt Liz also stated that I had to take care of myself and added they probably offered a payment plan. No matter what she said and how she said it, I could not convince myself to go, simply because I did not want to be in debt to anyone, especially a medical facility. The conversation ended with me telling her I was tired of struggling with a job and a degree. I told her it wasn't fair, and I refused to stay that way.

After my conversation with my aunt, I knew something had to change. How does someone spend that amount of money on a degree and owe more than they make? That was not how I wanted to live. I started to think of ways to make extra honest money. Going to a church where faith was the main focus, I began trusting God and paying my tithes. Tithes consisted of paying ten percent of your income, which is found in Deuteronomy 14:22 (KJV). When you only bring home about six hundred and fifty dollars every two weeks, tithing was not an option. When it was offering time, I would not use an envelope. Instead I put my two or maybe five dollars in proudly and returned to my seat. When I was in college I did tithe at one point, but that was a short season that changed quickly. I knew I could do it, but it's different when you have to pay rent, lights, and water. Making that decision came with some hesitation, but I needed to do it, so I did.

I began placing my ten percent in an envelope along with a whole lot of faith. The bills seemed to tower over my responsibilities, but at some point, I had to get out my slingshot and fight a whole new giant. Tithing would be a true test of my faith and a chance for God to show Himself strong in my life. The first month was super hard and frustrating, even after the bills were paid. There was no extra to do anything with, but I had enough faith to believe that God would feed me and put gas in my car. Coming home from work and having no idea what I would eat because the grocery store was not an option and my refrigerator and cabinets were bare, was a true test of my faith. Halfway through the month I didn't have anything but a can of sardines and a few eggs, so that was dinner for two days.

Testimony service was an important part of the service at church. That was when we were able to tell about a test that we overcame, how God made a way out of no way, or even how we were healed from a disease. Listening to the saints tell their stories encouraged me to hold on. When I went to work I would try to work through my break, so I wouldn't be hungry, and lunch would go by quickly. My coworkers were sweet and very supportive; however, I never told them what I was doing, mostly out of embarrassment. Usually we all met in the break room and chit chatted about life, relationships, and whatever other topic landed on the table during that hour. One particular day one of my coworkers came in with a gallon-size Ziploc bag full of corn dogs. I thought to myself, *What is she doing with all of those corndogs?* She held them up and said, "Me and my husband can't eat all of these and I thought you would like to have them." My eyes began to well up with tears because I knew I didn't have any food at home, but once again, God had a ram in the bush just like He did for Abraham in Genesis Chapter 22. I was shocked, or should I say impressed that God thought about me. My coworker had no idea that I didn't have any food at home, so I knew this was all God. No one else knew my situation, but God knew and he told me to trust Him enough to get everything I needed. I wanted to call my male friends to supply what I needed and every time I started to dial their numbers, something would happen, and I couldn't speak to them. God kept telling me to trust Him, and no one else and He would take care of me. Eventually I listened to Him, especially after the corndogs incident, and He continued to come through for me. As Christians we should trust God completely, with no hesitation. The label of trust issues seemed to wrap itself tightly around my body to the point I was gasping for air. The day that label began to release its hold was when I began to trust God with my finances.

LABEL 22

No Determination

That summer there was a television show out called Rich or Poor. The host was very famous and popular, and I loved it; the show was a hit. In the middle of the summer, I decided to go back to Indiana to see my family, friends, and goddaughter. During my visit I got a call from an old church member and she told me she was working downtown for the Rich or Poor auditions. I was shocked and excited. She said, "You should come down here." At that moment I was not really busy, so I decided to go, and stand in what was probably a mile-or-two-long line to audition. When I got there the line was about four blocks long, but I chose to stay. I had never auditioned for anything in my life, but I knew I wanted to give it a shot. It was a hot day in the middle of August and there were thousands of people waiting for this opportunity just like me.

Standing in a long line was not fun, but the people around me made the best of it. As the line moved forward, I talked with the other wanna-be contestants to pass the time. After about five hours of standing in the sun with nothing to drink or eat, I had very little energy. The line finally moved to where we were inside the building and it was such a relief. The staff of the show made it fun once we were on the inside. The room before the audition room had a huge stage in it that held about six or seven hundred people. People who were auditioning provided entertainment by rapping, singing, dancing, and performing any talent they had. The room was hot, but more bearable than it was outside. We had to be in that area for about another hour, and the next stop was the audition room.

After the long wait, it was finally my time to audition. All of the potential contestants were separated into smaller rooms about the size of a small office. Once I was placed in that particular room, there were two other people in there with me, so they literally could hear my audition. In each room there were two people who were already in the room, one of which was the camera person and the other was someone who told you what they wanted you to say. I was so nervous because even though they told me what to say, I had to provide the expected delivery of what they wanted me to say. The gameshow staff wanted me to say my name, occupation, age, and where I am from. After I delivered the basic required information, the rest of what I wanted to say was up to me. The difficulty was I only had thirty seconds to audition. I just thought of something quick, but I knew it was not my best. The casting manager said that if I made it to the next round, I would receive a call the next day. Waiting has always been difficult for me, but I waited the entire next day and I received no call.

Rich or Poor was doing casting calls all over the country, so I searched for another opportunity to audition. I was shocked to find that the next audition was only about two hours away from where I lived. That made me extremely happy and excited. The next audition came with a little more preparation and knowledge about what the show was looking for. I knew that this audition would literally make me or break me. It was the one chance I had to get out of poverty. Creativity and excitement was what I needed to get a callback.

The whole two-hour drive there I was praying and asking God to give me what to do and say. I made the drive by myself, because no one else wanted to get up that early or stand in line in the hot smoldering sun for just a chance and not a guaranteed spot. It was the chance of a lifetime and I needed to nail it. As I pulled up to the audition, the line was at least one mile long, and again, it was ridiculously hot and humid. Standing in the line for four or five hours, gave me the opportunity to meet people and learn about who they were. No matter how much people talked to me and I entertained it, I stayed focused. I had one agenda and that was to make it on the show. While waiting, I still had no plan of how I would kill the audition, but I just had to do it.

Years prior to the audition, I had decided to go natural and not put any chemicals in my hair to straighten it. My hair was in its natural state and in a nice big afro that consumed so much space, it required its own zip code. My afro was off of my shoulders and got many touches, stares, glares, and created a few conversations. As I stood in line it hit me all of a sudden: I could do something with my hair that was going to be creative and absolutely bizarre. Standing in line the only thing that I had was a bottled water that was now hot water due to the heat, and my purse. I needed to put on my thinking cap, my creative cap, and any other kind of cap instantly. The line was getting shorter and shorter and I still did not have a plan. Looking all through my purse to find some type of prop to use in conjunction with my hair was not looking promising at all. However, growing up in poverty had its advantages. It taught me how to use whatever I had to make it work. At that particular moment I needed to go back to my childhood and improvise. My MacGyver spirit kicked in and I came up with something.

The moment finally arrived. After all of the anticipation and waiting, I was in the building. Once again it was time to show the casting director what I was made of. This time the setup was a little bit different. They put us in a very large room with about thirty cameras set up on both sides of the room. Each camera had three people doing their auditions on one camera, so you had to really shine. I am naturally loud even when I'm not trying to be, so when there is a million dollars at stake, I have to be extra loud. I wanted to stand out, be remembered, and heard, so I forgot about my inside voice and gave it all I had.

The camera that I was assigned to had one of my new friends from the line on it as well. He was an older black man who wore tethered jeans, a worn t-shirt, and a faded baseball cap. During the coaching for the interview, the shows' staff stated that I had to say my name, where I was from, and what my occupation was. The man in front of me stated with a very calm and monotone voice that he was a retired school teacher from Kentucky and his name. In my opinion his interview was boring and plain. Now please don't forget there were about ninety to one hundred people gathered in a room standing in front of the cameras, not to mention the people before you and after you. It was my turn to do my thing. I thought about every speech competition, play, and recess that I ever had in my life. I was determined I would not be the fallen star who did not get their fifteen minutes of fame.

My plan was to put paper, pens, money and cards in my hair and pull them out as if I was searching for numbers. I stood in front of the camera with my professional Speech team voice to give my name, occupation, and where I was from. Then before I knew it, I became an actress playing the part of a fifth grader on recess with her friends. My adrenaline was pumping out of control. This would be the most crucial half minute of my life. I began screaming, using my hands and afro to make it happen. I thought to myself, *if they don't choose me, they won't forget me.* Out of nowhere a rap came out of my mouth and my props were flying out of my hair, I felt like no one else was in the room and I was center stage on Broadway. The rap shocked me because I have never had any rhythm and I only knew to make the last word of each sentence rhyme, so that's what I did.

The staff and the entire room had come to a standstill and watched as I completed my audition. One of the ladies who I stood in line with was on the other side of the room at a different camera. She saw me as I was walking out and stated, "I couldn't even do my audition because you were so loud." I know she thought we were friends and best buddies, but that was not true. We just stood in line together, that was it. My response was, "Well I'm sorry, but there is one million dollars at stake and I had to do what I had to do." Her facial expression said it all. She walked away with a major attitude and was not smiling. Leaving that audition felt amazing; I did feel a little bad about disrupting other people's chances, but I had to bring everything I had. This was my second chance to change my life, so I took advantage of it.

Just like the week before, I waited for my callback the next day. That audition went so much better than the first and I knew they were going to call. When I went to church the next day, I even prayed and asked God to have them call me back. The whole day I held the phone in my hand, even during service, awaiting that life-changing call. After our regular service at church, we had to drive to Memphis, Tennessee to attend another church service and I must admit, my faith that they were going to call was dwindling. Our service got out at about 1:30p.m. that day and the drive to Memphis was about an hour and a half away. The car I was in was packed. Zakeya's family was in the back and I was in the front while she drove. We talked about the audition, service, and just everyday stuff, so the ride was going by quickly. We were about thirty minutes away from our destination and my phone rang with a number that I did not recognize. At that moment, in the midst of someone's sentence, all I could do was scream while looking at the phone. Something just told me that it was someone from the show calling, but I was so excited all I could do was scream and look at the phone. Zakeya finally screamed out, "Answer the phone, it's them." When I answered, anyone watching would have thought

I had it all together. Somehow, I was able to put on my professional voice that was a little animated and say hello. After answering the phone, the casting director confirmed I had been chosen to go to the next level. Yes, the screams started all over again with excitement. She gave me a list of things I needed to do and get for the next day, which was shocking, considering it was a work day and I would have to take off.

She instructed me to fill out an application, get people to do a mock show, and drive back to the place where I auditioned. Confused about why I needed some of the things she requested, I just rolled with it and didn't ask any questions. She explained to me the next audition would be more personal and they wanted to know my story. Once I got to church, I started recruiting people who could possibly take off and go with me. Yes, the choices were slim because it was such short notice. The service we went to was short and we were able to get back at a decent time. The people that I had recruited all got together and had a poster party. I went to the store and we got markers, poster board, tape, glitter, anything to make poster boards and we made some that looked amazing. The posters were bright and had sayings on them. My favorite poster was a drawing of me with a big afro and items sticking out of it just like at my audition. Someone in the group came up with the idea of a slogan, which I thought was genius. As we thought about it for a couple of hours, we decided the slogan was going to be, "It's all about the 'fro." By the end of the night we had a full jingle, posters, and a whole cheerleading squad to help cheer me on.

Sleep was nowhere near my house that night; I was overjoyed. The process was really just getting started, so I had to keep up the excitement. I kept telling myself, "I got this far, so I can keep going." The funny thing was some of the people that were going to the auditions with me had never seen the show and had no idea of how to play. On the ride down, we were trying to explain how the game worked and what the point of the show was. We laughed so hard because one person could not get the concept. The closer we got to the second audition, the more nervous we all became; we finally just said, "Follow everyone else's lead." Once we arrived there were a few other people and their supporters as well, so the nervousness soon increased. Although the casting director explained what to expect, it was pretty much forgotten upon arrival. While waiting for our turn, we could hear people screaming and laughing and truly enjoying themselves. My team began to have a prayer meeting, practiced our song, and continued to try to explain the show.

Sitting in the waiting area for my name to be called was the longest hour of this journey. The casting director came to get me first, then sat me down in front of a camera and interviewed me. She asked why I wanted to be on the show. I told her something like it's my favorite show and I shared some of my story with her about how I grew up poor and the struggles I'd had. She also asked me what I would do with the money if I won. I explained to her I had a new car, just a few months old, but it did not have power locks or windows. She seemed really surprised to learn I was so basic and really didn't want much. My main goal was not to struggle financially. At that point I had struggled my entire life and it was time for it to be over. While I was in my interview, I became very personal and shared the real Ryda. It really grabbed at my interviewer's heartstrings because she made the statement, "No one would be able to tell that's your story. You're so happy and cheerful." I told her, "Yes, you just have to push through, and understand that things will get better sooner or later." My interview went well, and I was pleased with my performance.

After my interview, the staff called in my group of supporters. When they entered the room all I heard was yelling and screaming like no other. Everyone in the room was caught off guard except me because I knew what we came to do. I knew it was going to be interesting because everyone still wasn't sure how the game was played. I was even more nervous than I was in my interview, but I had to come all the way with it. At that point it was now or never.

To my surprise the area where my supporters and I met was set up just like the set of the show. I really didn't know what to expect, but I knew a mock game would be played. The goal of Rich or Poor is to win as much money as possible, the most being one million dollars. There are models holding cases that have numbers on them, and no one knows how much money each case is worth. The cases hold values from one dollar all the way to one million dollars. The contestant has to choose a case that becomes their case, and that case will remain on the stage with them while they play the game. The contestant has to choose other cases throughout the game, hopefully choosing the case with the least amount of money in it. Every time a case is selected, that money will disappear off of the board. Once the box is picked, the "banker," who is unknown to everyone, will offer you a deal for your case. If the amount he offers is too low, you say, "Poor," if it is an amount that you agree with, you then say, "Rich."

Following the audition, the waiting game began, and it was a long one.

Remember, the auditions were in the summer and the first time I heard from the casting director was late September. That was a total of about two or three months and the timeframe was that short only because I called her. To my surprise she answered the phone and we had a good conversation. I felt good about it, but she never really confirmed that I made it to the next step in the process. My patience was wearing thin. By then it was the middle of December and persistent me called her again. I'm a firm believer that if you want it bad enough, work hard for it and it will come to pass. That conversation was a little different than the previous. My hair was my ticket to fame, because I based my entire audition around my long thick, tight, curly, afro. Most Caucasian people don't understand the work it takes for black people's hair to become what it is. That day I was irritated with my hair and wanted to put chemicals in it to straighten it and I explained to her I just wanted to know if I needed to wait. Her response went something like, "I just left out of a meeting and they were talking about you; please don't do that. If you don't hear anything back from me by March or April, please call me." This was the best news yet, although it was just January.

LABEL 23

Poverty

One Friday night in January, about two weeks after my last call with the casting director, I was lying down after a rough week and my phone rang. It was during the time when minutes on a cell phone were limited and would not become "free" until 9:00 p.m. If you went over your minutes, the charge was fifty cents per minute, so most people would not use the phone for about a minute or two waiting until the minutes renewed. Yes, I was also guilty of that and was not ashamed of it. When my phone rang that night, I only had about four minutes left until my cycle changed on Sunday. I did not want to answer for two reasons: one, I had no minutes to spare and it was only about 8:00 p.m. and two, the call showed up as a private number. Something told me to answer it, so I did, and my life changed forever. When I said hello, the voice on the other end said, "Hi, may I speak to Rita?" I responded with "This is she, who am I speaking with?" I was half sleep and worried about my minutes, so I needed to get straight to the point. She said, "This is Sarah from Rich or Poor." I thought there was no way it was finally happening, and I just knew someone was pranking my phone. I told her, "Stop lying, this ain't funny, my minutes are running out." She said, "No really, I am the producer and the casting director gave me your information." I rose up out of that bed like my name was Lazarus out of the bible and questioned her some more. I just knew my friends were pranking my phone because they knew how excited I was about this opportunity. I asked her one question that would seal the deal and it was, "What was my casting director's name?" When "Maria" left her mouth, I knew the call was real, and I started screaming and jumping all around my house.

Sarah told me she saw my audition and was excited about working with me. When she said that, I started to scream all over again, with no restrictions. Naturally, I can be overly dramatic and can become excited over the smallest things, but this was huge, so I was on ten with excitement. After I calmed down, Sarah had the chance to speak to me about her real purpose for calling. I still could not believe this call was happening even after I expected it. Have you ever wanted something so badly and you knew it was going to happen, but had no idea when it would happen? That was the feeling I had at that moment. It was my biggest answered prayer to date. I knew out of the thousands who auditioned, I got a call back. God is real.

That call changed a lot of things in my life and my perception of the things in it. The way I viewed Jesus changed; I understood that if He could do this for me, I needed to become a part of His DNA and stop being a foster child. This meant I needed to be covered by His blood and accept that He just wanted me. At some point in your life you've got to understand that no matter the struggle, hardships, labels, disappointments, or neglect, if you survived the next second, you are loved. Jesus was showing me that He loved me. No, He didn't have to do this for me, but He did. There were so many times I prayed and questioned whether or not my prayers made it to Jesus and not just out of my mouth. Although this was just the start of the entire process and Sarah assured me of that through the conversation, there were no guarantees I would be on the show, but I was still excited.

The process of being on the show was about a month long. Sarah stated in our first conversation that we would become best friends and that we did. I am almost positive I spoke to her at least five times a week about my likes, dislikes, supporters, wardrobe, and even my 'fro. Some of the conversations were short and some were extended, but I enjoyed every last one of them. In my opinion, the most difficult part of the process was having them choose my supporters. It seemed as though every person who knew I existed wanted to accompany me on the show. The only part I played in choosing my supporters was submitting names. Everything else was left to the producers and their team. Rich or Poor needed people on the show who were outgoing and could hold the nation's attention for an hour. My personality is so big; I didn't have a problem doing it. However, some of the people on my supporter list were not as, let's say ... enthusiastic as their friend. Most of the people in my life are the opposite of me and Sarah and her team found that hard to believe, since I am an extreme extrovert.

My friends and family were calling me every time the show would contact them to see if I knew the inside scoop on who they would choose. Everyone was waiting in anticipation to see if they were among the chosen ones. Sarah really would not ask me anything other than how my relationship was with the potential supporters. The show only allowed three people to go on with me, so it became a time when my phone was ringing off the hook. Everyone who the show contacted was calling me asking me questions that I didn't know the answers to. I wanted to know just as badly as they did, but I had to wait as well. The time finally came when I knew who was going to join me on the show and I will admit I was not disappointed. I would have loved for Tasha and William to be selected, but the ones they chose were still good. From the time I was selected and with constant phone calls from Sarah, I got little sleep because I was so excited. For about two weeks I did not sleep a full night. The thought that I could change my economic situation was overwhelming. I would toss and turn all night and would not be tired when it was time to wake up. One night I tried everything to get back to sleep and could not, so I called my Aunt LaLa. I would say it was about two or three in the morning and let me tell you, she was not happy. When she initially answered the phone, she thought something was wrong since it was so late. I explained to her everything was fine, I was just excited about the show and couldn't sleep. In her exact words she said, "Girl, you better go take some Nyquil and stop calling me in the middle of the night." I cracked up laughing, because I kind of expected that response, but thought just maybe she would entertain my excitement. We laughed and got off of the phone. She even told me she loved me, which meant she really wasn't mad.

The time came when Sarah told me who they wanted to be my supporters on the show, and I must say I was really okay with their choices. Their final selection included Zakeya, my longtime childhood friend Ellis, and my cousin Stephanie. I was so excited to have these three women, who have actually known me for years by my side as I made some major decisions. Zakeya was probably the most excited and kept my adrenaline pumping, mainly because I saw her practically every day. Ellis is a very cool individual but can easily become excited and being on national television made her come out of her shell a little bit. Stephanie is very quiet and is more rational and will think her way through and won't act on instinct. All three of them are different in many ways, but they all had my well-being and best interest at heart. I must say I had some really great "supporters" who were ready to help me in making the biggest deal of my life.

About a month after the initial conversation with Sarah, the arrangements were made for me and my supporters to fly out. Zakeya and I flew out of Tennessee, Ellis at the time was living in Iowa, so she flew out of there, and Stephanie had just relocated to Alabama and that's where she came from. The show was taped in Los Angeles and none of us had ever been there, so we wanted to enjoy it even if it was only for a day. We all arrived at different times and were pretty much tired from traveling; however, I did manage to see everyone that night. The excitement was in the air and we all had on our game faces. We came ready to win. Our emotions were all over the place; nervousness, fear, and being completely overwhelmed, was running rampant through us.

Of course, I could not sleep that night at all, but I felt that the sacrifice of a sleepless night was worth what was to come. I prayed and asked God to give me favor and I believed that He would. It was time to get up and head out to the studio with all of my supporters. The show had a van pick us up and it was a very awkward ride for me. We all tried to mask our feelings, but with an elephant that big, it needed to be talked about. The closer we got to the studio, the more silent we became, surprisingly enough.

Each one of my supporters played a special role during the show. Zakeya was the one who prayed no matter what, if I forgot to acknowledge Jesus, she would. Ellis was the risk taker. She would push me to the edge, and make sure my parachute would fly open at the last second. Stephanie was my logical and safe reasoning, reminding me to make good choices and not to go too far. All of these ladies balanced each other out and I needed all of them throughout the show. The moment came when we reached the studio, and the reality sank in for me.

Once we entered the studio, things were crazy and nonstop. We were introduced to Sarah, who was so happy to finally meet me in person, since by then she knew me and all of my business. We also had to go to wardrobe and get our hair and makeup done. Whenever I'm nervous I make jokes and laugh a lot, so let me tell you the entire team at Rich or Poor was cracking up. None of it was fake; the staff was really sweet and kind, so it was genuine fun. After all of the logistics and the paperwork we had to fill out, it was show-time. This was the moment that I had been waiting for the last couple of months. The wait was over, and it was time to rock and roll.

The show was not based on academics, common sense, or any skill I could use. Most people would say luck, but I knew it was nothing but prayer that got me through.

Before I was strategically placed in the audience, I had Zakeya pray for God's will to be done. At that moment I trusted God more than at any other time in my life. I knew He would show himself strong and would keep His promise to me. I sat in the audience until the host called my name. My nerves were completely gone, I was shaking, praying, and sweating as I sat there. The host called my name and there I went running down to center stage and all eyes were on me. I kept telling myself, "Ryda, have fun and be you." The host literally introduced me to the world and the show officially started. Please remember that I was a young woman who struggled financially her entire life, recently started paying my tithes, and had to ask my landlord if I could be short on my rent in order to have enough money to go to California for the show. The first offer that was made to me during the show was under twenty thousand dollars, and unlike most of the other contestants, I had to think about it. To me that was a lot of money I was turning down, knowing that I was broke, busted and disgusted.

I have a huge personality and I let it all out during the show. I laughed, cried, sat down, ran, hung out with the models, some of everything. The models even came out with pink afros, to honor my afro. The models really enjoyed wearing them and we had so much fun with the pink afros. The host became my best friend and assisted me with any instruction that the producers gave me, since I was so overwhelmed and couldn't focus. About midway through, I finally relaxed and had the best time that I'd had in a long time. I told the world about the struggles I'd had financially and even stated that my furniture was in bad shape, including the fact that my chair was without legs and sitting on the floor. Being transparent was what made the audience, staff and even the host fall in love with me. The only thing I wanted was money to get power locks and windows for my vehicle and new furniture. Other contestants' wish lists were dramatic, and in most cases, not realistic. The audience knew I was just a down home honest woman trying to make it.

The show had progressed to a point where it had become difficult for me to make decisions because the money had increased. I wanted to take everything that was offered to me every time; however, I had to keep going until I felt comfortable walking away. My supporters made sure I was comfortable with every decision I made. They told me to keep going, slow down, or suggested that I take the deal. The lights were bright, the crowd was loud, and the money was increasing rapidly. I felt like the show lasted for hours and took me the entire day to complete. Getting to the final deal took a lot of patience and prayer, but we finally got there.

I was offered four hundred and two thousand dollars with only a few cases left, including the case I picked. I had no idea what I was going to do and was completely confused about what my decision should be. During that moment I gathered all of my supporters around in a circle and had to get everyone's thoughts on what I should do. The audience on all of the other episodes that I watched would always encourage the contestants to keep going and take the risk. My audience was different, they pleaded with me to take the money and go home with that amount. I stood there, and I looked around at the crowd and people were crying, pointing their hands towards me like they were praying, and yelling, "rich, rich, rich." The chant became so loud and encouraging, I ran up to the buzzer and pretended that I was going to keep going. I looked over at the host and his face looked like he'd seen a ghost when he thought I was going to keep going. He was not allowed to give me advice, but his face said it all. As I continued to hear the entire crowd chanting, I pushed the buzzer and ran over to my supporters screaming and jumping.

The tears began to flow, and I could not stop thanking God for the biggest blessing of my life. God had just blessed me with four hundred and two thousand dollars, and I was in complete shock. When the show ended, the host pulled me to the side and told me, "You deserve all of this, you are by far my most favorite contestant ever." This was very humbling for me, and definitely put a smile on my face that this famous host of the show would say this about me. The emotions of being nervous and afraid immediately turned into shock, joy, peace, and happiness. As we walked back to the room for a quick post show interview, I stopped everyone in the hallway and told them about my show. They were there and witnessed it first-hand, but I wanted them to know that I was just happy. At that very moment I knew my life would change.

The show had ended, and it was time for all of us to get back to our regularly scheduled lives. While in Los Angeles, we had time to go to the mall and do some shopping. Once we were finished, Stephanie was the first one to have to leave for the airport, so she rushed back and departed. As the rest of us hung out at the hotel, Stephanie called and said something happened to her flight, so she would be leaving early the next day. By the time Stephanie got the news, the staff from the show had left and could not transport her back to the hotel. After speaking with the assistant for the show, she assured me if I paid the thirty dollars for the taxi ride, they would reimburse me. I went ahead and paid for the taxi fare for Stephanie to get back to the hotel that night. Normally, thirty dollars would not be that big of a deal, but money was tight, and I wouldn't get the money for being on the show for ninety days.

The next day we all headed to the airport to go back to our home states. Having the chance to see my friends and family was a great experience, but the true challenge was ahead of us. While at the taping of the show, we had to sign a waiver stating we could not tell anyone any details about the show, including how much I'd won. This was so difficult because everyone knew I was going to the show and the first question everyone asked me was how much I won. Typically, I am not good at holding things in like this, but it was mandatory that I did for a whole month. The visit to Los Angeles was in February and my show would not air until March, so we had to keep it a secret for a long time.

When it was about a week before the show aired, my coworkers and I decided it would be a great idea to have a viewing party. Getting a place, food, and party favors was easier than I expected. I was able to rent a room very cheap, a local rent-to-own company let me rent a sixty-inch television for about twenty-five dollars, and coworkers and friends brought food. The last thing on the agenda was to invite people to come, which was another easy task. The list of guests included coworkers, friends, and church members. My mother did not have adequate transportation, so I knew she was not going to be able to attend, but she did host her own viewing party at her house. Since the party was on a Monday, Tasha was not able to get off of work. William was invited and much to my surprise, he drove from Indiana to Tennessee to attend the party.

Everything was in order and on May 5, 2007, it was time to see the show. Things were set up in the room and there were about fifty or so people who showed up, including a reporter from the local newspaper. It was a very exciting moment for me as well, because even though I knew what the outcome would be, I didn't know what part they would show. I was on set for about three hours, and the show had only aired for about forty-five minutes. The show was on and you literally could have heard a pin drop at the venue. Things were so quiet until the host said my name, and then my guests went crazy. As the show progressed, my guests were on the edge of their seats in anticipation. People were screaming and yelling like the show was live, and it was so much fun. There were so many high fives, chants, and screams; it had their adrenaline pumping and they had no other choice but to join in.

The night ended, and people were shocked about my four-hundred-and-two-thousand-dollar blessing. My phone was ringing non-stop, text messages were like short stories, and my guests wanted pictures and autographs. It felt so good to be able to share with the people around me what I had experienced. My Aunt Liz called me and said that she was at my mom's trailer with about twenty or thirty people watching the show, and the excitement was so intense the whole trailer was shaking. Next my Aunt LaLa called, and she was just peacock proud of her niece. During the conversation she said, "Girl, I'm famous, too." My response was, "How, Aunt LaLa?" She said, "Girl, I know you and you're famous now, so I'm famous." Both of us laughed so hard, and I said, "So now you're famous by association?" She said, "Yep."

Going home that night was different from any other night in my life. By the time I got off the phone and settled down, it was way past midnight. The only thing I could think about was *What in the world am I going to do with my money?* One thing I knew for sure, I was going to pay my tithes, which was ten percent of the four hundred and two thousand. God blessed me beyond my pint size cup and the blessings overflowed. Realizing this, I knew I owed God. If nothing else was paid, my tithes were going to be paid with no hesitation. Laying in the bed was the only thing I could do; I was still in disbelief. That night I managed to get a couple hours of sleep.

Even though my show had aired, there was still a ninety-day wait before I received the check. That morning I had to still go to work and needed gas before I went. The show aired on NBC, so everyone in the entire country who watched Rich or Poor that night saw me. In my opinion my days were still the same, going to work, attending church, and just living my normal life. It never really dawned on me that just like Aunt LaLa said, I was famous now.

As I stood at the gas tank the morning after the show, there was an older Caucasian woman standing on the other side of the pump getting her gas. Minding my own business, and thinking I needed to hurry up so I wouldn't be late, out of nowhere I heard a small voice singing, "It's all about the fro." Looking around confused, I was trying to see who in the world could be singing my song. Lo and behold, it was the lady at the pump. I looked at her for a second, and after we made eye contact, she started to sing it again. She smiled and stated, "Oh my God, I loved your show, honey. You deserve it." Again, it still did not register that hundreds of thousands of people saw me just the night before. Still in shock that this lady loved my episode, I just smiled and said, "Thank you very much for watching."

The day after the show I called Sarah to remind her of the thirty dollars she owed me for Stephanie's cab ride because I needed it. Sarah assured me that I would receive the money by the end of the week, and I was satisfied with her response. Friday after work I came home and there was a FedEx package left on my doorstep. I was happy because I knew it was my thirty dollars.

As I walked into my house I received a phone call, and while talking, I opened the package. Pulling the check out, I saw it was not for thirty dollars, it was for three-hundred-and-seventy-seven-thousand dollars. The screams just started coming out of my mouth, and I had to get off of the phone. My eyes were wide with disbelief. The game show winnings came four days after the show aired and not the ninety days they told me. It was late Friday and the bank was closed, so I called Zakeya and she was in shock as well. We discussed what I needed to do with the check until the morning and I did just that. My next phone call went to my pastor, and I asked him to pray over the check and to ask the Lord to give me wisdom on how to use it. My pastor willingly prayed as I asked, and I waited until morning came. That night I slept with the check under my mattress and I didn't leave the house for the entire night.

That Saturday morning, I woke up ready to take the check to the bank. Once I got dressed and headed out with the check, I shut the door behind me and headed for my car. When I went to get the keys to unlock the door, I noticed I had locked my keys inside the house. I could have fainted. Because it was a Saturday, the bank closed early, so I had to figure out how I was going to get a hold of my landlord and get to the bank on time. After trying for hours to reach my landlord, I was finally able to track him down and he opened the door. The issue was the bank would close in twenty minutes.

I called the bank to ask them if they could wait for me to get there in about ten minutes. The bank employee said they would close and if I didn't make it, I would have to make my transaction on Monday. This made me super nervous. I told her I had to open up another account and I really needed to do it that day. She reiterated that they would be closing soon, and they didn't do new accounts on Saturday. The only thing I said to her was,

"Look, ma'am, I am the lady that was on Rich or Poor. I have a check for three-hundred-and-seventy-seven-thousand dollars and I need to handle this today." There was no more discussion. She said, "Ms. Percy, get here as soon as you can. We will wait for you."

When I arrived at the bank, it was about five minutes before closing and when I left it was about two hours later. They wanted to know about my experience on the show and we laughed and had a good time. The check was deposited, and I was happy about them waiting for me.

About a week passed and my popularity gained momentum, which caught me off guard. Everywhere I went people wanted a picture, my autograph, and would scream shout outs. My fans expressed to me that they loved my realness and referred to me as a cousin or girl next door. Little children were star struck when coming in contact with me, which melted my heart. At that time in my life I felt like Oprah's baby cousin. I was a local celebrity and I loved it. No matter where I went, people recognized me, even out of state. When I went on vacation, people were chasing me down to get pictures and autographs as well. Remaining humble was the key, anyone who asked, I gave pictures and autographs. One of the most excited fans that I ran into approached me when I was in Vegas. She was one of the ladies who was in my audience. She recognized me and expressed how much she loved being there and that I had kept her on the edge of her seat. People began to stop me so often; it was difficult to just go to the store or out to dinner. My fans were everywhere. While driving through neighborhoods they stopped me in the middle of the street. High-fives, fist pumps, and hugs became a part of my everyday life.

LABEL 24

Sickness

I began my journey into womanhood (started my cycle) in the fourth grade at the tender age of nine years old. My cycles were always painful and uncomfortable with a lot of bleeding. They were very heavy and went on for as long as two months straight with no break. I went to doctor after doctor and there was never a cure or solution for the issue I was having. The doctors tried to put me on birth control, but the pills made me sick and I vomited until it was out of my system. Vomiting is like death to me. Every time it happens, I cry uncontrollably, and it takes me a while to regroup. When that time of the month came, I fought through the pain and tried to keep a normal life. Masking physical pain is always a task for me, but I did it; otherwise, I would be out of commission until my cycle ended. The pain was absolutely unbearable; if I had to relate it to anything, I would say childbirth, although I've never experienced it. Women I know say childbirth is close to death, and that's how I felt at least half of the month.

In April of 2008, I had a bad health episode that was painful and sent me to the emergency room. I was in excruciating pain in my abdominal area that brought me to tears. I have always had pain right before my cycle, but I couldn't tolerate it this time, and I needed help. Living by yourself makes being sick even more difficult. You have to make the decision alone who you should call and what to do when help shows up. Since I was still fairly new to the area and I had been attending the church, I called a sister from the church. She was so nice and sweet. She came right over, took me to the emergency room, and stayed with me until I was able to go back home. That was another example of the love the saints showed to each other in a time of need. The end result of that visit was a suggestion to contact my doctor. Normally I would have just listened to that advice and kept it moving, but due to the severity of the pain, I contacted my doctor immediately.

When I contacted my doctor, she instantly suggested I have a hysterectomy. I can remember sitting in the chair feeling numb, and unable to move anything but my mouth and when it moved no words rolled off my tongue. The doctor stated that she saw multiple tumors and she thought a hysterectomy would be the best way to go. That procedure was not an option for me, because I hadn't had any children yet. One day I knew I wanted to be a mother to a child that I assisted in creating. How does a young twenty-eight-year-old with no children avoid having such a serious procedure done? The only thing I could think about was my future and I knew I had to see if there was another option.

After much prayer the Lord revealed there was another option for me that would reduce the pain and other issues. It was a different surgery that would give me a chance to give birth. That sounded so much better than the earlier option and gave me some peace. At my age I had never stayed in the hospital overnight or even been attached to an IV. I must admit I was so afraid. I didn't like hospitals because of what happened to my mother's husband. He had gone into the hospital for an illness and never came out. He literally passed away in the hospital. The thought of going into a hospital terrified me; although I knew God could take care of me, I was still very afraid.

The night before my surgery I didn't get any sleep; I tossed and turned the whole night. Although my relationship with my mother was not like the typical mother-daughter relationship, she did come and support me during my surgery. It was nice having my mother by my side. The church members and the pastor where I was attending were right there as well, and when I came out of surgery, I asked for my pastor. My pastor was supportive in most cases and his presence was not a surprise. During that time, it was very important that I had a strong support system.

After the surgery I needed to be off of work for six weeks to recover. Zakeya and her family opened up their home to me for a couple of weeks. Zakeya is very motherly and was a great help. The hospitality they showed me was so gracious and warm. Her entire family pulled together to make sure I felt comfortable. The girls gave up their room, provided breakfast in bed, they even made sure I made it to all of my follow-up appointments, and everyone catered to me as if I were in a five-star hotel. My healing was in full swing and I did not have any setbacks.

When I was cleared by my doctor and able to drive comfortably, I went to Indiana and Kentucky to spend time with my family. During that time, I sat back and reflected on my life and how things could be better. Even though physically I was improving, something was still missing. Every human being is entitled to a peaceful life, and I desired that as well. Money was no longer an issue for me due to my winnings from the show, but something else was missing. While with my family something triggered in me that I needed to focus on my spiritual journey as well.

While recovering fully from my surgery, not only did I spend time with my family, but I also spent some intimate time with God. That was life changing to me because I could clearly hear the voice of God and I wanted to be obedient to what He was saying. The outside of me was coming together, but my inside needed some work and the touch of an interior decorator named Jesus. The pastor continuously talked about the Holy Ghost and how He resides on the inside and He gives you the power to overcome sin. That was what I was missing, He should be on the inside to put the final touches on my life.

In August, there was an older lady in our congregation who had terminal cancer. The pastor's wife asked all of the women to go on a week-long consecration for her. I willingly participated in the fast and knew that I needed it. It was designed for someone else; however, I believed God enough that I could get the residue from the miracle that was coming. The fast was called, and completed, but I continued on. While on the fast God spoke to me and said if I kept it going, He would give me the Holy Ghost. That was not hard for me to do at first because I wanted what everyone else had. When the members of the church went through trials, they seemed to do so without effort. Witnessing the saints overcome life's speed bumps with a smile was amazing to me. I knew the fast would do me good, not just spiritually but naturally. People equate sickness with something physical, but in this case, I was physically sick and spiritually sick. I wanted what they had and when I questioned any of them how they did it, their response was always the same, "It's the Holy Ghost."

When I told the Lord I would fast until I was filled with the Holy Ghost with the evidence of speaking in tongues, I did not know how long it would take. The saints told me that I needed to let go of everything that was holding me down, taking my peace, and creating a disturbance. Doing that would be difficult, because I had trust issues and I had things and people in my life holding me back. The process became real, my prayer life was on point and so was my determination. One thing that I was afraid of was letting go of people and losing the men that I had unholy relationships with. Staying focused on what God ordered me to do was the goal and I knew it would be all right. When you are obedient to what God says, everything will work out in your favor. The people and the men that I wanted to get rid of just started falling off without me saying anything to them. It was a sign that I was doing something right; they just started walking away. When they left, it allowed me to get in position to receive what I needed. Many would say it was a curse, but it really was a blessing. From that I learned that sometimes you have to get in the place where God needs you to be, so He can speak to you in silence with no distractions.

LABEL 25

Government Housing

While I was on the fast, I also was encouraged to buy a house. At the age of twenty-eight, I decided it was time to make the purchase since I was able to financially. My list of wants wasn't extensive, but it was specific. My list consisted of three bedrooms, two full baths, a two-car garage and an open kitchen. Houses were going fast at the time and the realtors were busy, but I did find a realtor I liked. At times I don't think I was her favorite client, due to me having a hard time finding what I wanted. We looked at tons of houses all over the county and the city, but nothing I fell in love with. Frustration soon set in; I just wanted to find a nice place to rent. This label seemed like it would never come off, no matter how hard I tried to rip it.

I was on the verge of giving up when my realtor called me one day and said, "I have a house that I think you will love." Reluctantly I agreed to see the house. Following behind her, I became even more concerned because we'd looked at houses in that neighborhood before. When my house hunt began, my friend William told me to always look at the meat of the house— the structure and not the furniture, paint, or any personal things. As we pulled up I did like the outside, so my attitude got better about the house. My realtor opened the door and once I got past the dark paint, worn carpet, and the overabundance of wall hangings, I was excited.

My realtor looked at me and saw that my eyes had lit up; she smiled because she knew this could be the one. As soon as I got to a computer, I sent the link for my potential house to Zakeya, William, and Tasha. The pictures were not the greatest and the décor choice of the current owner did not help.

The house wasn't dirty or disorganized, it just had a lot of stuff in it. I wanted Zakeya and her family to see it, so I scheduled another viewing. The moment Zephaniah, Zakeya's husband walked in he was disappointed, only because he could not see the meat of the house. Regardless of anyone's opinion, the house met all of my wants and needs, so I wanted to make an offer.

The realtor was ecstatic that all of her hard work and time was not in vain, and I'd found my house. I put in an offer and it was accepted for a price lower than it was listed for. My closing was scheduled for the Monday before Thanksgiving, a very busy week of the year. I could not wait for the closing to happen, and when that day came, I took my time and read over the paperwork before signing. When I left the closing, I asked my pastor's wife, Zakeya, and a prayer warrior to come by and pray over my house. When they arrived every room, closet, and exit was covered in prayer. As they prayed, my spirit went into a state of gratefulness, my words would not form and release from my mouth. When I was in college, I had a conversation with Ms. Thomas about becoming a homeowner before I was thirty years old. At that time, I was not sure how, when, or if it was going to happen, but there I was, twenty-eight years old, standing in my house with the keys.

Closing, keys, and prayers were completed, soon the hard work would begin. Paint was first on the list of things to be done to the house. The painter that I hired was quick, professional, and reasonably priced. His only request was for me to purchase all of the materials and he would take care of the rest. The decisions that I had to make about the colors were difficult, but I did it. While at Lowe's getting painting materials, I met a contractor, and eventually hired him as well. The painter was so eager to finish the job in a timely manner, he worked on Thanksgiving and it was not required for him to do so. He finished the job and my house looked so different, it was warm and more welcoming. Next, it was time to get the contractor over to put down new flooring, install updated lighting, and appliances. The company that completed the work did not disappoint either. Finally, I had to purchase furniture for every room except the spare room. I was not a pro at decorating, but William specializes in home décor, I called and texted him more times in the month of December than I had the entire nine years of us becoming friends. William was very supportive and helped me turn my house into a home. My home was complete in about two months after closing and that took a load off my mind. Although I had won a lot of money on the show, the label of poverty did not get ripped off until I bought my home.

LABEL 26

Uncommitted

Now that the house was where I needed it to be and comfortable, I still needed something else in it. One month after I moved in, I felt the house needed a little extra character. I wasn't sure what it was, but something was missing even after the pictures were hung and the furniture was in place. One cold night I ventured off to Treasures and as I was leaving, I saw a man sitting in his vehicle near the door, holding something wrapped up in a blanket. I assumed he was waiting for his wife. He held it like it was a baby, but it was way smaller than that. I walked up to his window and asked what he had. He said, "Oh, it's our new puppy." My eyes lit up as bright as the Treasures sign. She was so little and cute. I asked the man where he got her, and he gave me the contact information. As soon as I made it back to the house, I called to see if there were any more puppies. The lady who answered was also the breeder and she said she had one more left. I told her I could meet her after work the next day to pick him up.

The next day arrived and Zakeya's girls Uriah and Unik went with me to pick him up. The girls were probably more excited than I was about the new puppy. Since I wasn't familiar with the area where the breeder and I originally agreed to meet, we met at a gas station on the highway. There was not much thought or wisdom that went into this on my part. She told me he would cost a hundred dollars and we could make the exchange at the designated meeting spot. Come to think about it, it was kind of like a drug deal. I didn't even see the dog because he was wrapped up. She gave me the blanket, I gave her the money and we parted ways. Riding back with a brand-new puppy and two preteen girls was very entertaining. Unik, the youngest, asked the question of the night, "So what are you going to name him?" My response was, "Baby, I have no idea, I need ya'll to help me." After that comment was made, the thirty-minute ride back was filled with laughter and memories that will never be forgotten. Since the puppy was black and white, so many names were blurted out, such as Patches, Socks, Prince, and every other cute name you could think of. I dropped the girls off and there I was with a nameless dog who didn't have any food, toys, or crate.

There was only one other person in my life who had small dogs and that was Ellis. I knew she would know exactly what I needed to do and get. I called her on the way to Treasures and she gave me a list of things to get, specifically what kind of food, toys, size of crate, and even shampoo. The puppy was so tiny he fit in the palm of my hand, so I told Ellis I was afraid he would get lost in the house. She stated, "That's an easy fix. Get a cat collar that has a bell on it, so you can hear him." In my opinion that was an absolutely brilliant idea, to put a cat collar on a dog. While in Treasures, I was able to look at him in better lighting and noticed he had a royal presence about him. I continued thinking about a name and the name Prince stuck in my mind. That was the perfect name for him. Once we got everything from the store, mommy duty started. As soon as I got home, I got everything situated and knew that this was going to be easy. He would sleep, and the night would be peaceful.

Well, if you have ever been a new parent, you know that was not realistic at all. That night was tough, and I decided as soon as morning came, he would be homeless. Nothing was working out in my favor with Prince. He ate and drank, but that was it. He didn't want to be in his crate, so I put him in the bed with me. I didn't feel comfortable with that because I didn't want him using the bathroom in my bed. If I picked him up, he was okay; when I put him down, he cried. Not having had any experience with human children, I had no idea what to do with this boy. I needed him to understand that I had to be at work the next morning and if he didn't take his little self to sleep, he was going to need to look for a new mommy. Finally, I wrapped him in a blanket and he cuddled up next to me for the night, after about two hours of trying to get comfortable. I figured all of the chaos was from him missing his birth mother, and I wasn't sure how to comfort him.

After the first night he became comfortable with the house and began to roam freely. That meant having accidents in the house and sleeping anywhere he wanted to. The first full day of having Prince, I made him a doctor's appointment to get checked out and it went well. The only concern of the doctor was that he wasn't completely weaned from his mother, which I discovered the night before. According to the doctor he should have spent two more weeks with his mother, but due to the Christmas holiday, and probably because the breeder needed some extra cash, she let him go early. With Christmas coming in two days I needed to find someone to watch him, so I could spend the holiday with my family in Indiana. The joy that came from a good visit was cause for a photoshoot to welcome him officially to the family. Of course Zakeya agreed to keep Prince and the girls were so happy. Since I didn't have any children, I was constantly being asked when I would have children. That year I made birth announcements of Prince for all of my family and friends for Christmas.

Driving to Indiana I had many thoughts about my new baby that left me uneasy. I started to question whether or not it was a good idea to get a puppy since they required so much attention. One thing was for sure, I knew he was in good hands with Zakeya and her family. The day after Christmas things went wrong quickly; Prince became very ill and I was six hours away. I gave Zakeya permission to take him to the doctor, and she did. The next day he got sick again and after Zakeya did all she could do, she took him back to his doctor. This time he stayed overnight because he was just too much for Zakeya to handle. My trip was cut short and I rushed back to Tennessee. The doctor said his sugar levels were low, but he had an easy solution, which came in a clear glass bottle called corn syrup. Things began to look up slowly but surely, but the first month was filled with trips back and forth to the doctor with little to no sleep. Every time I would think to get rid of him, he would do something cute and a whole day would go by.

I have never been an animal person, but Prince changed my attitude. He was so lovable all he wanted to do was be held and have his belly rubbed. We would go everywhere together; if he heard the word bye-bye, he knew it was time to go. He was getting so used to going, when he saw me grab his blanket he would beat me to the door. Prince only weighed a pound, so he could go everywhere with me and no one ever knew I had him. I was respectful of people eating, though, and never took him to a restaurant. People loved to come up and pet him, and he loved them doing it. When Prince was a few months old, I took him to Treasures and put him in my purse just like we did all the time, but this time was different. Prince discovered he could bark at people and get a reaction from them, so that's what he did. When we were just about done shopping, the store manager approached me and told me that I couldn't bring animals in the store unless they were service dogs and I needed to leave with the dog. Needless to say that was our last trip to Treasures together. Prince became a part of my everyday life and I treated him as if he were a child. He could understand and would listen to everything I would say and react to the command. Prince really taught me commitment and how important it is. I have always thought I was a fairly responsible person, who was committed to anything I accepted; however, Prince introduced me to a new label. In addition to introducing me to the label, he also assisted me in ripping it off.

LABEL 27

Unsaved

Becoming more and more faithful to church services and ministry, I could see the change in me. I was in the second month of the fast and loving my transformation. The fast was working, but there was still one thing I didn't understand and that was how God could be Jesus too. The Apostolic faith referred to it as the Godhead, which meant there are not three Gods, but God is Jesus and Jesus is the Holy Ghost. While sitting in Sunday School for the review, one of the sisters quoted the scripture John 1:1-2 and John 1:14 and this gave me the full understanding of the Godhead. The bible is the truth and it will change your life and your mind. John 1 states that, "In the beginning was the Word, and the Word was with God, and the Word was God." I was so intrigued by that verse. Then she recited John 1:14 and it said, "And the word was made flesh, and dwelt among us …" Many scriptures were quoted regularly during services, but Jesus used that one to save me. I believe the reason it was so effective was because of the fast, which made me more sensitive to God's voice.

Shortly after the life-changing scripture was revealed to me, my church hosted a revival. During the revival I wanted to get the Holy Ghost, so I was focused and ready. There I was sitting in service, listening to every word the guest evangelist had to say and letting it minister to me. When the service came to an end, it was time to go up and get prayer and seek the Holy Ghost. I am pretty sure I was the first one at the altar. Service after service I went up and nothing. Finally, I changed my mindset and attitude about it. I said to the Lord, "Jesus, if this is real, fill me up just like you did everyone else."

It's customary to go to the altar and lift your hands as a sign of surrender. When coming to Jesus you need to give up everything that you know and allow Him to take over your actions, thoughts, mind, and rip the labels off. I lifted my hands, then the guest evangelist came over to me and laid her hands on me to pray. I told her I needed the Holy Ghost, and she said, "You have to believe." She also asked me if I had been baptized in Jesus' name and I told her, "Yes, nine months ago." She looked me in the eye and said, "It takes nine months to deliver a baby, what are you waiting for? It's delivery time." I closed my eyes with my hands lifted and began to call on Jesus. Before I knew it, my tongue changed, and I was speaking in tongues. Oh wow, I thought, this thing they had been telling me about was real. All I had to do was be obedient and believe. Three months of fasting and getting myself together had actually worked. It was the best feeling ever, nothing that I had ever experienced in my life could compare to Jesus living on the inside and the evidence that filled my mouth.

At that point I felt like I could do and be anything I wanted. Throughout my life I had experienced failures, victories, and everything in between. Everything that I had to go through in my past was worth letting go and trusting Jesus enough to take over my very being. Rich or Poor was a big deal, but receiving the Holy Ghost was even bigger. My life changed from that point on. There was a glow about me that I could not explain, but I was shining so brightly. Even though I was happy, it was awkward sharing the good news with my family, mostly because they thought that since I went to church, I was already heaven bound. Being an example and allowing the people around me to see the change was more important than anything I could tell them. It felt good not being a part of the groups, sin, and situations I used to put myself in.

After experiencing my new saved life, I wanted to do more. Living life to the fullest has always been my priority. I have a heart for youth and knew I was a born leader. There was something inside of me that wanted to find more programs for the youth in the community. Living in Boonville for five years, I noticed there was nothing for the youth to do but sports. Sports programs are good, but not all children wanted to be on a field or court chasing some type of ball. Some children like to experience the arts or even some STEM activities.

Not knowing how I could make a difference, I prayed and sought God and He gave me an idea. The idea was so crazy that I did not share it with anyone for months because I knew people would laugh at me. Personally,

I was embarrassed and had no idea how I would even be able to make it happen. When God gives you something, He will also give you the confidence and instruction to go with it. Once God gave it to me, I began to have dreams about what He told me to do. I tried to block it out, but it wouldn't leave my thoughts.

LABEL 28

Follower

Every morning I would watch Good Morning America before I went to work and one particular day a story aired that grabbed my attention. There was a young man who was elected mayor in Oklahoma at the tender age of nineteen. That was the moment when I knew that I had to step out on faith and do what I was told to do. The dreams, conversations with Jesus, and ideas about being a leader were confirmed. That was exactly what God told me to do. I questioned His directive many times before attempting to move forward. How in the world was I going to be the mayor of any town, city, or county?

The most I ever did politically was vote. I took pride in voting because of what my ancestors endured in order for me to have the right. I was the least likely person to attempt running for office, and to be honest, I didn't know if I was Democrat or Republican. What could I do to get the ball rolling on becoming a mayoral candidate? Speaking with other politicians in the community was a great start, but I knew I needed to take it a step further. I called the mayor of that city in Oklahoma. I told him I saw his story on Good Morning America and I needed some tips. He actually talked to me about his journey and gave me some ideas on how to be successful. Now was the time I could share my vision with people and not be concerned about their opinions.

Of course the first person I had to share it with was my favorite and number one supporter, Zakeya. Initially she looked at me with a bit of confusion, then she said, "Oh my, that's wonderful. I think you should go for it." One thing I know about her is she is always going to tell me the truth, even if it hurts my feelings. When she gave her approval, I had to let other people in my life know before I went public. Next on the list Tasha, William, family, and friends needed to hear the news. Everyone who was close to me was very supportive and on board with my outlandish ideas.

One of my college friends, Brielle said to me, "Wow, Ryda are you serious? You're the only person I know who does whatever comes to their mind. First you move to Tennessee without knowing anybody there, then you get on Rich or Poor, and now you're running for mayor. I have a lot of friends who are doing great things, but none of them are running for mayor. I am so proud of you, girl; you're doing it." Brielle also complimented my new saved life and told me she could see a difference. She told me that her boyfriend said, "Ryda is truly saved. She knows the word and lives by it." That conversation ended with a huge smile and a thank you. My team is amazing, and I love them. I appreciate the way they love and support me. None of my true friends doubted my ability or skills to do this with class and be victorious.

Doing my research about the politics in Hamilton County, Tennessee I learned that there were two mayors. Each city had a mayor in the county, and then there was a county mayor. I opted to be a candidate for the county mayor position. I knew the work would be strenuous but doable. Going into politics, I felt as though I had three strikes against me. I was only twenty-nine years old, about to turn thirty. I was not only black, but I was a black woman. The third strike was that I was not a native of the county. I knew those barriers would play a part, but I never allowed them to be the basis of why I was running, or why I should win. Since I was running for county mayor I was responsible for campaigning in the entire county, not just the city of Boonville. Hamilton county had had the same mayor for many years and he never had an opponent run against him. He never put up anything to campaign with: no signs, shirts, or ads because there was no competition, so he didn't have to. The current mayor was elderly and had a good relationship with the residents—everyone loved him. This was going to be a huge task, but nothing that Jesus and I could not do.

First things first, in order to get on the ballot, I had to get a petition with about two hundred signatures from registered voters in the county. The community was small and had about thirty-seven thousand residents living there. People see me as an individual with a big personality, but that's not always true. While I do have a big personality, I get uncomfortable easily when I am not in a familiar environment. I felt it would be challenging to get the signatures because I did not really know a lot of people.

Small towns are very family oriented and if you didn't grow up there, you became an outcast. Praying is always my go-to when I need some help, so I prayed and asked God how to get the signatures. My first stop was to the members of my church. The members all signed the petition willingly and were excited about my decision. The signatures from church made a dent, but there was still work to do. From that point on I went into businesses, stopped people on the street, and called everyone I knew. Mission one was complete; all of the signatures were in before the deadline. Next I had to get my name on the ballet and let people know I was running.

April was the month I started cracking down and laying out a plan on how to execute the victory. That would give me four months to prepare before the elections in August. I needed shirts, business cards, postcards, yard signs, newspaper ads, anything that would help get me and my agenda out. April was a busy month for me, filled with many decisions. I started going to all the events in the community and making myself known. The community was shocked and could not believe that I had the guts to run, especially against my opponent. Some of the people were very supportive, others turned up their noses, rolled their eyes, and even mocked me.

Even my opponent became very rude and disrespectful at public events with hundreds of potential voters around. If there was an event and both of us showed up, I made it my business to always acknowledge him by his title and shake his hand. I quickly learned that he was not fond of me and did not want anything to do with me. A couple of months in, he even went so far as to call me, "the little black girl that was on the show." Yes, it was hurtful, but I still needed people to see the love of Jesus on the inside, so I smiled and treated him with the utmost respect. He would ignore me, refuse to shake my hand, and pretend as if I did not exist.

Determination was the key to a successful campaign, and it would get me through. Never in my life have I quit at anything, and this election was not going to be an exception. Right before early voting began in July, the Republican Party hosted a forum for all of the candidates. Initially, I was not invited, but the day before the forum I got a call inviting me. I felt that would be the best time to share my platform and tell everyone why they should vote for me. Some may think it would be easy to go and present, but it was not that easy. The lady who phoned me asked me to come, but when I said I would, I could tell she thought I would say no. She clearly did not want me to attend. She thought I was going to say I could not make it and she began telling me why I shouldn't go. She explained to me that she had no control over what would happen at the forum and added that some very popular individual really did not want me to speak.

Throughout the whole election, this was the first time I recognized that I was disliked primarily because of the color of my skin. Later she told me that I could come, but I had to stand at the door to hand out business cards, and I could not do it during the event. By the end of the conversation, I felt belittled and beyond mad. I expressed to her that I was very upset, that I would be contacting someone about this matter and I would like to decline the invitation. After declining, I finished my day at work and went home.

Shortly after I got home the representative phoned me to tell me that she felt bad about the situation and how I was treated. She told me that she fought for me to get the same opportunity at the event as other candidates. That did bring some excitement and I agreed to speak; however, I was still disappointed about the situation. Agreeing to speak at the event meant I had to prepare a speech that would really grab the attention of the residents and win their votes. In my heart I knew that I would not be respected, but I knew I had to try even with the wall of discouragement in front of me.

The next day was the event, and I was so nervous. I never like to base things on my feelings, but the way I was treated left a bad taste in my mouth. Upon arriving, Zakeya and her girls came out to support me, and it was great to be able to see some familiar faces. I looked around the room for my opponent and found he did not show up, but I did notice his wife was there. Out of all of the thirty thousand plus people who lived in the county, with thirty percent being African American, only two showed up outside of my support team. That truly surprised me, especially considering one of the attendees was a candidate himself. It was clear that this was not the place I should be, but reciting the scripture, "God has not given me the spirit of fear ..." I held my composure, put my feelings to the side, and patiently waited for my turn to speak. At this point in the race no one had really heard me speak in a formal setting, but with my education and experience, I knew they would be in disbelief.

So there I stood before a room of about two or three hundred people with only about five who looked like me; I had to show up and show out. As soon as I opened my mouth, the crowd was very attentive. Some even took notes, and others looked on with curiosity. Every other candidate that spoke before or after me focused on growing up in the area and their family history, which was not the meat of my speech. My goal was to share why I was running, why they should vote for me, and the way I could better the county. One subject I touched on heavily was the youth and finding more activities other than sports for them to get involved in.

Anytime I speak I always attempt to get the audience engaged. The question I posed to this audience was, "How many people in here have investments such as stocks, mutual funds, IRAs, etc.?" They looked at me, thought about the question and began raising their hands one at a time. The next question I asked the audience was, "If you invest, you expect a return, right?" Their hands went up again in agreement and this time they were accompanied with a few smiles. That broke up the stiffness that was in the room, body language became more inviting and I became more comfortable. Once they answered the question, I expressed that our children are our future, they are our investments and the only way we could get a great return is if we would invest. I expressed to them it was easy math: the more we invested in our community, schools, and youth, the greater the return would be.

I closed my speech and took my seat. Immediately after my speech I heard the audience clapping, but when I looked up from gathering my things, I saw people standing up and clapping. All of my nervousness and unfair treatment was worth it, any bitterness I had went away. Seeing many of the people standing after my speech, let me know I had just nailed it.

Once the event was over an older white man, who was at least in his seventies, approached nervously. Even though I felt as though it went better than I even expected it to go, I was still on guard. The man was nervous and seemed to be unsure of how to approach me or even what he should say. When the man opened his mouth, he introduced himself to me as my opponent's campaign manager. Immediately after the introduction I began to put up every wall I could reach for, but with a smile. I stood in complete shock, not able to think what he was preparing his mouth to say. He looked me square in the face and said, "I am truly impressed, you did an amazing job on your speech. Way to go and keep it up." That was one of the best compliments of the campaign.

While I was campaigning so many women told me that they were going to vote for me and they were proud that I had the guts to run. Children were so excited, especially the black children, to see someone who looked like them doing something seemingly unheard of. It gave them hope to achieve their goals. My campaign started just two years after Mr. Barack

Obama, was the first African American to win a presidential election in 2008. That motivated me so much that I went for it. In all of my thirty years I never thought that I would ever see anyone that had pigment in their skin get elected to the highest position in the United States of America. If Mr. Obama could do it and break through barriers, and I know the God that I serve is not biased, I knew He could do it for me too.

The week before early voting, I hosted a meet and greet for the community. Since I am creative and wanted to do something that was out of the box, I had to come up with a theme. After much deliberation with Zakeya and William, I chose to do a Hawaiian Luau. The luau, took a lot of work and planning because I was still knocking on every door, going to events, all while still having to go to work every day. The event had to be huge and my goal was to have hundreds of people attend. Running for office is very expensive, everything costs, nothing is free. There were going to be fees that needed to be paid from the advertising, food, and venue. Surprisingly enough I did have people who donated more than just money. People began stepping up, donating their time and supplies for the meet and greet.

I told my family in Indiana about the event and to my surprise they came. My mom, aunt, youngest brother and his family, cousins, Tasha and her children and even her mom all came to support me. Ms. Thomas was not able to come but she did send a couple of made-from-scratch cakes for the cake walk, and William sent a financial donation as well. Having my family and friends there made everything better. It's a wonderful thing to be supported by people who love you. Love is an action word, and on that day, I knew I was loved. People showed up from all over the county, with anticipation of meeting me. The event had to be one that would be memorable and go down in history as one of the best. During the event we gave away door prizes, gift cards, leis, and so many other items to promote my campaign.

After all of the activities were over, my family and friends hung out and enjoyed each other. Reflecting on the day and just being family. Later on that day my mother told me how happy she was that she could make it. That brought joy to me, the fact that she enjoyed herself and her time in my space. My mother is sensitive, but not a touchy-feely person. There has never been any doubt that my mother loves me; I believe she just does, she just does not know how to show it. When my mother and I were finally alone, she expressed how proud she was of me and stated, "There is no doubt in my mind people will vote for you and you will win." My eyes began to well up with tears because this was only the second time in my entire life that she told me how proud she was of me.

Once the meet and greet was over, it was time for the actual event, and things began to get more and more hectic. The campaign was heating up and early voting had ended. August had finally arrived, and election day was in five short days. The pressure was on. My team and I hit the pavement harder than ever, going to events, knocking on doors, and soliciting votes. The night of the election I knew I wanted to have a party to celebrate not only the victory, but also the journey. With the election being just a couple of days away, I reserved a community center in advance for election night. Throughout the journey, I made my mind up that no matter what happened, I would walk away with experiences I could take with me to reach my final destination. I knew I had done all I could do and gave one hundred percent to the campaign.

On September 4, 2010, one day before the big day, my nerves were shot. It seemed as though support had grown overnight, and people expressed to me that the county needed fresh, new ideas that were beneficial for everyone. Being humble throughout the campaign was key, even when people wanted me to act out of my character. My mind was racing, and my focus was on winning what I had worked so hard for. The race had become more difficult as time progressed, but it was worth it.

LABEL 29

Failure

September 4, 2010 arrived with short notice, but it was time to see how desperately this county wanted change. That morning was a little different than most other mornings on the campaign trail, not bad just different. There were a million and one things to do and I made sure I was able to do them all. I made sure to request a day off from work, so I could take voters who did not have transportation to where they could vote. Voters had my cell phone number, so they could call if they needed a ride. I went and picked them up, took them to vote, and then took them back home. I also had to get the food and decorations ready for the reception. Needless to say my adrenalin kept me moving because I was operating on little to no sleep and it had started to take a toll on me. I was ready for all of it to be over, so I could get back to my life, Prince, and sleep.

The time came for my friends to gather at the center and learn the results of the election. None of my family was able to make it, but I had a good support system. My friends Zakeya, her family, church members, and other supporters from the community all came out to support me. As tired as I was from the day, God gave me the strength to entertain all of my guests and do it with a smile. Soon the votes began to come in. Yes, my nerves were completely on edge. My guests were just as anxious as I was to see the final results. While at the party, we were listening to the radio and every time the host on the radio show mentioned the mayoral race, the room became silent. The first round came on and I was in the lead. Oh, the cheers that erupted from those early results. I was so happy and felt good about that round, but that was just one set of results. The next four rounds produced a different sound that consisted of comments like, "It's ok, it's not over yet," "There's still time," "You did really well, you broke through walls." Eventually the crowd dispersed and so did my efforts to win the race. Of course I was not happy about the results; however, I was happy with my decision to run.

Once I got home it all hit me like a ton of bricks. Even though I was tired, my mind was racing and reflecting on every door I knocked on, every hand I shook, and all the people I met during the experience. I sat on my couch alone while Prince sat on my lap and one lonely tear fell, then another, and another. My entire face was wet from the defeat I'd experienced. It was a defeat I did not want to accept, but I knew it would make me better and build more character. To be honest, it made me feel like I was a complete failure; I was ashamed, and embarrassed. It was like everything I'd worked so hard for was for nothing. Going into this race many people were against me, so I knew it would be tough. I just wanted that sense of accomplishment, and it did not come.

My phone was ringing off the hook with people from all over wanting to know the results. Some calls I took; some my voicemail took. The one call that I was shocked by and happy to take was the call from my oldest brother. He explained that he had been listening to the results and knew I did not win, but in his eyes, I won. That meant the world to me. Sometimes you have moments in life where you look through your rearview mirror at your past and see how many successful miles you have gone. Well, that call from my brother was at that moment in my rear-view mirror. That call made me realize that I had more courage, tenacity, and heart than most people and I can do anything in life that I want to do.

LABEL 30

Fear

The following year went by, business as usual, until my employer was the victim of cuts. Earlier that year I had a petition before the Lord that I wanted to move out of the city. I was not sure how it would happen, but I laid it before Him and forgot about it. I worked for the government, still doing the revised Welfare-to-Work program, and I knew at any time budget cuts could happen. There were three of us who ran our office and our bosses and supervisors were forty-five minutes to three hours away. It was not uncommon for the supervisor, president, and vice president of our company to show up at our office at the same time. That particular day all three of them showed up and no one thought anything of it until we all were called into a meeting. As every meeting started out, it was calm and relaxed, this one was no different. We laughed and told stories, nothing serious at all. Then all of a sudden, the president's whole demeanor changed, and we knew it was serious.

All three of us sat in anticipation of what she would say. You could tell in her non-verbal communication that she did not want to share with us. She got herself together and told us that due to budget cuts, one of the positions would be eliminated. That meant that one of us would soon be without a job. Of course the management team felt bad, but none of us became distraught. After the meeting was over, I told Zakeya that I wouldn't apply for the available positions; I felt she needed it more than me because she had a family. Much to my surprise, she said she did not even want it because she wanted to start her own business. Instantly, I knew I had to get my house on the market and look for a job outside of the town I was in. At some point in our lives we know that some people, places, and things are for a moment and not forever.

My life was about to change, and I did not know how or when, but a major change was on the horizon. I had about four months to find a job and sell my house. Selling a house is just as stressful as buying the right one. The realtor that assisted me in purchasing my home was the same one I used to assist me in selling it. She came over one afternoon after work and explained to me the things I needed to do and how much I should list it for. The price was agreed upon and so were the changes, and the house was officially on the market in March.

When the house was first placed on the market, there were a lot of potential buyers, but eventually the number of buyers slowed down. That was the moment my faith had to kick into overdrive. At that point I had about two months left to sell the house and find a job. I became worried. My goal was to move to Nashville and start a new career and life in that city, but God sometimes has a plan that doesn't line up with our plans.

The search was on. I applied for job after job in Nashville and did not get one interview. I decided I would look in other cities in Tennessee, but never did I think to look in another state. My cousin Sean and his family had just relocated to Ohio on the other side of Cincinnati, and after a conversation with him, he suggested that I go there. I was open to going anywhere at that point because I was not getting any callbacks for jobs in Nashville.

Time was winding down. The end of June had made its entrance and it was my last day on my job and I still had not sold my house. Applying for jobs became my part-time job; it was time consuming and overwhelming. Questioning whether or not I had made the right decision began to eat at me. Every Sunday I went to the altar to get prayer for a job and to sell my house. There was one job that I applied for in Northern Kentucky that was about forty-five minutes from where my cousin lived. When I spoke to the woman in human resources, she said that she may have something come open in about a month, so I held on to that. My faith was shaken and tested but God remained faithful through it all.

That summer right after my last day, I went to visit my cousin in Ohio. My plan was to take interview clothes and just show up at the place where I had a potential interview. Since I was six hours away, it would save me a lot of money if I could interview while I was there. I felt it would be a long shot because I had not spoken to the lady in HR in a couple of weeks, but it was worth a try. Literally every piece of faith that I had kicked in and reminded me that God is in control. As I drove I prayed and asked God to show me favor while I was in Ohio. My cousin and friends questioned my motives and suggested that I at least call to see if an interview would be possible. Ignoring everything everyone suggested, I wanted to stick to what God had promised.

During my drive God repeatedly told me that he would take care of me and stop worrying, so I did just that. From Tennessee to Ohio my GPS took me through Kentucky, there is a bridge that connects the two states that is about a mile long. While driving across the bridge, my phone began to ring from a number I did not recognize, but it came up as Kentucky on the caller ID. It took me by surprise, but I answered, and it was the lady who I was going to see the next day. When she said who she was, I had to take a deep breath and get my thoughts together. I wondered how in the world that could happen at that particular time. My only answer was God is an on-time God.

The conversation went well, and she wanted to set up a phone interview since I was about six hours away. When she found out I was in the area she was excited and gave me a time to meet with her the next day. I agreed to the time of the interview and the first person I called after hanging up with her was my cousin Sean. When I told him what happened, he said, "No way, are you serious?" He was in just about as much shock as I was in, but he was happy for me. Going to visit my family, I had some expectations to look for a job and possibly interview, but I never expected things to work out the way they did. The rest of the day was fun and because it was the exact same job I did in Tennessee for seven years, I didn't get nervous at all.

Coming from a small town and not truly being exposed to a lot of traffic, I knew I would have to get up early to get to my interview on time. My cousin lived on one side of Cincinnati and the interview was on the other. Getting up that morning was not a problem because I was excited about the interview. My cousin explained to me that traffic would be horrible, so I left about two hours early to ensure that I would be on time. He was right, the traffic was backed up, but not as bad as I thought it would be. I arrived about thirty minutes before my interview, still excited and ready to take on the day. The interview was with the man who would be my supervisor and his supervisor, and I still did not get nervous. The interview went very well, and I felt good about it when I left. The first person I called was my cousin and I told him I got the job. He was surprised because he could not believe they offered it to me so quickly. I explained to him they did not offer it to me yet, but I felt good about how it went, and I knew they would offer it to me. My faith superseded all doubt and gave me peace.

I was so confident I had the job, I began to look for housing when I left the interview. The area was fairly big, with not just one large town, but multiple smaller towns. I did not know which areas were good, so I drove around for about four hours, looking for a reasonably-priced but spacious apartment for Prince and me. I was heading back to Tennessee that day, so I knew I needed to find something before I left. The moment I was going to give up and try to schedule another time to come back to look, I drove past a complex that caught my attention. It was an older complex, but it looked nice, clean, and safe, so I stopped in to look at one of the units. The goal was to get a townhouse or something that had a private entrance. When I pulled up, I noticed there were some townhomes on the property, and that made me so happy.

I took a deep breath and entered the leasing office to find a middle age white woman who was dressed properly and was friendly. She greeted me with a smile and a lot of personality, which was comforting to me. She asked me what I was looking for and when I would be ready to move in. My situation was unique because I had not even had a job offer, but I knew it would come, so I had to prepare. Explaining my situation to the leasing manager was easy and she understood. After about thirty to forty-five minutes of chatting, she showed me a townhome that I fell in love with. There was going to be a bit of an adjustment moving from a house that fit a family, to a townhouse, but I knew I could make it work.

When I left the property, I got right on the highway because I knew I had found a place to live. My search for a new apartment had come to an end after visiting that property. That trip really paid off in more ways than one and mentally I was ready for the change. Cardinal was an hour and a half from where I was in Northern Kentucky and my Aunt LaLa still lives in that city, so I was going to stop to see her on the way back to Boonville. Leaving Northern Kentucky, I was all smiles and filled with excitement because I knew a huge change was on the horizon.

Once I was about thirty minutes into my ride, I received the call that I got the position. It's difficult trying to keep your professional voice, drive, and contain your screams, but I managed to do it only for about ninety seconds. The moment I hung up the phone I went into a praise and thanked

Jesus for the opportunity and for what He was doing in my life. The drive to my aunt's house consisted of a lot of joyful tears that would not stop falling. God knows not only how to put the puzzle pieces together, but He creates them, so He knows that they will fit perfectly when the timing is right.

My Aunt LaLa was so happy to see me, but she noticed I was not acting like my normal self. She questioned what was going on, and with tears running down my face, I had to share my blessing with her. My emotions were on overload and I stood in awe of how God had just worked things out on my behalf. I have seen God move before and I knew what He was capable of, but the way He did it that time left me at a loss for words. For the next hour the only thing I was able to do was praise His name, the heavenly language known as tongues filled my mouth and I was in pure worship.

Sometimes you cannot wait until Sunday morning to praise the name of the Lord, you just have to do it right then and there. When my siblings and I were younger, my mother used to say wherever you show out, that's where you get the whooping. That particular moment of praise reminded me of what my mother said. God showed out while I was on the highway and at my aunt's house, so that's where my praise was released. Fear lifted its head a few times; however, my faith dominated my fear.

LABEL 31

Anxiety

Once I arrived back in Tennessee reality began to kick in, and the packing also had to start. That was difficult for me because I had never moved an entire house before, so I did not know how to move. When I moved into my house I only had clothes, a washer and dryer, a bed and a dresser. This move was going to require work, a moving company, and a lot of money. A lady that I became very fond of asked if I needed help, and of course I did not turn her down. People from the church and my friends helped me pack up my house and get ready for the move. When my friend from the bank showed up, she had pizza and drinks, and with about eight people present, we had ourselves a moving party. The funny thing about all of this was I really only knew two people who were coming. During the two weeks of packing, I also completed all of the required paperwork to secure the townhome that I looked at while I was there. God will provide you with help when you need it most, and from the least likely source. Who would have guessed taking care of business at a bank could lead into a packing party?

Game day had arrived, and the movers had backed their almost semi-size truck in my yard and began emptying out my house. Leaving what I knew to be home for the last eight years was difficult, but I knew it needed to be done. I have never been the type of person who depends on other people to make it. I take risks and follow the path that Jesus prepares for me. My feelings began to switch from excitement to sadness. This move was bittersweet. Prince and I piled up in my vehicle and set out on the five-and-a-half-hour journey to our new home. I pulled out of my driveway for the last time with tears in my eyes, but with faith that I was on the right course. At that point in my life I understood who Jesus was and that He had a purpose for my life. My story seemed like a sad song, but with the help of the Lord, it was turned into a joyous occasion. The trials that I went through prepared me for my destination.

The ride seemed to take far more than the five to six hours that it normally takes. The night before, I was up late trying to perfect the last few things to make sure we were ready to pull out as soon as the movers arrived. The house had to be in tip top shape because it was still on the market and potential buyers would be stopping in to look. We got about two hours from the new apartment and my eyelids developed weights and would not stay open. I decided at the next exit to get to a gas station, so I could get a five-hour energy drink. That energy drink gave me the boost I needed to get me through the rest of the trip. The tiredness went away, Prince was sleeping, and Marvin Sapp, the gospel singer, was encouraging me all the way.

I arrived at the new apartment and the movers began to remove my things from the truck and I moved things out of my vehicle. Exhaustion was not a strong enough word to describe my level of energy. The energy drink had done its job, but then I crashed after not being able to sleep a few hours after I lay down. The first half of the move was over; I just needed to fill out the rest of the paperwork for the apartment. While the movers were wrapping things up, I went to the leasing office and completed my paperwork. The leasing manager was there and again, was very sweet and professional. While she gathered my paperwork, I broke out in tears. it just hit me that I did not know one person in the place I had just moved, and fear set in. She was so sweet. She comforted me and told me to let her know if there was anything she could do to make the transition easier. The move did not come with regrets; it came with fear of the unknown.

Monday morning arrived, and it was time to report for my first day of work. Everything was great after my orientation. I met with my boss and he treated me to lunch, then we were off to where my office was located. We arrived at what looked like an old school building that had been converted into a building with multiple businesses in it. The building sat on the corner of what seemed to be a busy intersection, across from a restaurant and a small bar. We walked in the building and not only did it look old, but it smelled old … almost like there was a mold issue. After providing a little bit of history of the building and what all it housed, we got to my office.

My new coworkers welcomed me, but they seemed to be checking me out, trying to see if I would fit on their team. There were three other people who I would work closely with: two women and a man who all seemed to be close friends. Sometimes my personality is too big, and I know how important first impressions are, so I kept my excitement to a minimum. The most shocking thing about entering the office was I did not see one person with a permanent suntan like mine. Out of all of the clients and staff, there was not another black person in the office. That was when I began to have second thoughts. I immediately thought to myself, "*This may not work out for me.*"

There I was in Northern Kentucky, doing what I had been doing for years: serving all types of people from very diverse backgrounds and not one person looked like me. My first day went well, and even though I was a little skeptical about it, everything worked out. My first phone call was to Zakeya; I had to tell her how my day went. Even though it was the same job, the environment and expectation were different. I believe in motivating people to always give one hundred percent, even if they only have onions and lemons to work with. I believe you should always make the best of any situation and the best will be the outcome.

A month after I was in the area, my house was still waiting to be sold with no potential buyers. It was a late Saturday morning and as I was prepping to get my day started, I began crying out to the Lord. My house needed to be sold, so I would not be responsible for a mortgage and rent. The house had been on the market since late March and it was early September and I was still a homeowner and a renter. As I started to pray and believe God for a miracle, my phone rang, and it was my realtor. It was not uncommon for her to call to say she would be showing the house, but I needed this showing to be the last. After answering the phone, she could tell I had been crying and I explained to her I had been praying. Her response was, "That's great. We have someone who is interested, and they want to pay cash." Immediately I went into praise, thanking God for the phone call. Some may not understand this, but I was in the middle of praying when my phone rang, and I stopped praying because of who it was. Sometimes before we can utter the need, God will provide it.

The next call that I got from my realtor a couple of days later was that they wanted to make an offer. I did not accept the first offer, I countered back a little higher and they accepted it. My boss was understanding and told me I could take time off to handle my business, but the realtor told me that everything could be done over the phone, fax, mail, and email. The realtor sent me all of the required documentation and I returned them overnight to make the sale final. As soon as I received them I signed, and I put them right back in the mail on the same day.

Once the selling of the house stress was off of me, I could focus more on my new job and meeting new people. The best thing about it was I never paid mortgage and rent because of the timing. During my first couple of months I was able to find a church and that helped me stay on the right track spiritually as well.

LABEL 32

Unemployment

The following weeks that came were like riding a rollercoaster: one day it was good, the next day it was rough. One thing that I held dear to my heart was my relationship with Jesus. Being a working professional, I do understand that I have to maintain my professionalism while on the job, but I will never be ashamed of my God. God has been too good for me to be ashamed of who He is and what He has done for me. People will watch you to see what you are about, and this held true with a couple of my clients. Every day I had at least one client come to my office and ask me about my relationship with Jesus and I told them.

Our offices were all individuals; however, there were no ceilings. So imagine having a nice sized space that was personal and private to some degree, but you had tall cubicle walls to the ceilings. This made it difficult to have private and confidential conversations. My coworkers were nice, but I was not part of their clique. We would do lunch and talk at work, but that was really it. They would have what I would call secret meetings and when I walked in the room, all conversations would cease. They began to question, or in better terms, attack me for having different morals, values, and standards. Soon it got to the point where I began to get sick coming to work because of the stress of dealing with my coworkers. My entire life I never fit in, so I was ok with that, but what I wasn't ok with was feeling like I was walking into a trap.

The clients began to call me names, which I was ok with, but then I had a client push me and threaten to physically do harm to me. The policy was if this happened, they were suspended and not allowed on the premises for a few days, but my supervisor never backed me. One of my coworkers was disrespected by a client and that rule applied to them, but it was nonexistent in my case. Why was it that when my space was violated, there were no consequences handed out? Soon it got to the point where I hated going to work after about month five. I began to question my safety and my purpose for working in this position. When I accepted the position, it paid a little less than I was making in Tennessee and I was unhappy as well. I started looking for other jobs and even went on a couple of interviews, but I knew I could not jump out of the boat and drown. In my opinion, the workplace should at least be a safe place.

The job was really starting to take its toll on me; I could not trust the staff and the clients were extremely rude and disrespectful. My boss called me one day and asked me to meet him at the main office; he wanted to speak to me. I gathered my things and went to the meeting. Something about it was off, but I didn't get nervous. When I arrived the lady from HR was also part of the meeting. She explained to me that she heard I was talking about God, Jesus, and praying and in her words, "If I hear of you talking about your God, Jesus, and laying on hands, you will be fired." She also said, "I will be writing you up and this is just a warning."

In my many years of working at any level, I had never been written up or fired, so it took me by surprise. I did not get upset, I just responded with, "Okay." It amazes me how people will persecute and try to tear you down because of what you believe, but they can have their own ideas of life and we as saints of God are expected to accept them.

After my meeting and write up I isolated myself; I withdrew from my coworkers except for "Hello" and "Have a good night." When my clients would come in my office it would only be for a limited amount of time. My name, integrity, and character are important, and I did not want my job to interfere with my excellent reputation. When you are truly saved, you become a light and people follow the light that is on the inside of you. No matter how hard I would try to keep the clients out of my office, they would still have a desire to come in and talk to me. Most of the time when they came in, it was like a safe zone for them. They wanted to tell me about their barriers and then ask me how to deal with them and how to get a relationship with Jesus like I had.

One particular client had so many barriers it was unbelievable that she was even waking up to start a new day. She had recently been released from prison, so she had a felony which made it difficult to get a job. She had become homeless and was living with her cousin, whose home was infested with bedbugs. On top of all of that, she had two young children, with no car or money.

She busted into my office completely distraught, her eyes full of tears, screaming and upset. She always had a positive attitude, so I knew that something terrible had happened. After telling me that she wanted to give up, she said her son was continuously getting into trouble because his classmates were bullying him because he was poor and dirty and did not look like them. For the last five or six days in a row the school had called her to come and pick him up because he was fighting.

The main issue with her having to go get him was she was required by the state to do so many hours, whether working, school, or community service, in order for her to get and keep her government assistance. The first thing that came out of her mouth was, "Can you pray for me, please?" At that moment we went into another unoccupied room in the office that had a ceiling and I began to pray like never before. The thought that I would be fired or get in trouble did not cross my mind one time.

The following week I had to attend a seminar that my employer sent me to that Monday. The seminar was helpful, and I learned some things, but something felt off the whole day. My coworkers called me and stated that my supervisor was looking for me and thought I was a no call, no show. That threw me for a loop because they were the ones who had set up the seminar and instructed me to go. I called him, and his excuse was, "Yes, I just forgot. No worries, nothing is wrong." The rest of the day it was like the Lord was speaking to me about accepting His plan and that He had everything under control. After the seminar was over I went home and began to prepare for work the next day, and God's voice began to speak so loudly that Prince barking, children playing outside, and neighbors talking began to fade. The Lord told me to pray and get prepared for work tomorrow. Confused but obedient, I lay prostate on the floor and prayed. While in prayer I just kept repeating, "Jesus, I trust you." It was unclear to me what I was preparing for, but I knew the Lord knew everything, so I just did it.

The following morning, I got up like any other day and reported to work on time and ready for what was in store. As I sat down at my computer I was unable to log on, and when I asked my coworker if she experienced the same thing, she said she was able to get into the system. After calling the IT office and no one answered, it was clear to me in that very moment. I went into the hallway and called Zakeya and told her, "I think I am about to get fired." I explained to her that my supervisor had been looking for me the day before, my access to the system was denied, and told her about my prayer with God the night before. She gave me a scripture and an encouraging word, and I went back in my office. The moment I entered, I was greeted by my supervisor. He said, "Good morning, can I speak to you back here?" My response was, "You sure can."

I smiled and made small talk while we walked to our destination. When we made it to the empty office, I saw a big brown Coach purse at the corner of the desk. At that moment I knew my time had ended at that place of employment. We finally stepped into the office and the lady from HR sat in the chair behind the desk. Still smiling I greeted her and had a seat. She explained to me that she heard I had prayed for a client and I had agreed that I would not do that. I was still smiling and listening to what she had to say and nodding my head. The next phrase that she said was, "Ryda, this is not a good fit for you and we are letting you go at this time. Here is a box for your things." My smile got bigger and I looked at her and said, "Okay, I thank you."

I grabbed the box and went to my office and gathered my things. As I walked out of the office she was standing there and asked for the key. I handed her the key with a smile and said, "Thank you, thank you, very much. This is a blessing." The look she gave me was one I will never forget. She thought I was going to be upset and cry, but no. God had already prepped me through prayer the night before and I knew it was well with my soul.

After getting to my car, I gave God some praise for releasing me from that situation. No tears fell, no anger was in my heart, and I was not upset that I had just become unemployed. Of course, I called Zakeya and told her I had been fired. At first she did not believe me, but finally she did. Towards the end of the day everyone that I was close to knew I had gotten fired and was concerned, but I was not. Honestly, I was happy that I did not have to put up with unfair and biased treatment from coworkers, my supervisor, and the clients. Prior to that termination, I had been applying for jobs, but nothing was coming through for me. There was no job in sight, but I knew my experience with God said He would make a way.

Not being from the area and knowing very few people, the only help I had was in Jesus. The job search intensified, and my faith increased.

My position ended right around the time my cousin and his family were going on vacation. His middle son was not able to go, so that left a spot available that they wanted to fill. My cousin asked me if I wanted to go and I responded, "Yes," so quickly. I knew I was not going to be at work, so I could go and enjoy the beach and gather my thoughts. My friends questioned how I was going on vacation with no job. I just told them, "I serve a good God and there is no lack in Him."

The destination was Myrtle Beach, and all I was responsible for was my food. It was going to be so much fun. Babysitter for Prince, *check*, bags packed, *check*, a positive attitude, *check*. I love the beach; it is one of God's most awesome creations. Every time I go to a beach I have to stop and give reverence to God for His mighty works. It's overwhelming and I get emotional just thinking about it because it amazes me how the sky and the water meet and there are no trees at all. While I was in His presence, I began to thank Him for what He has done in my life. I have heard people say that there is no God, but how can they not believe when there's no way a man can dig a hole that big and tell the water when to stop? My first twenty to thirty minutes I had my own quiet time with the Lord to just commune with Him and get in His presence.

As much as I like the ocean I am not a fan of getting in it. I love when my feet are in the sand and the current washes up on them. Swimming is not enjoyable to me, mainly because I don't know how to. One day we were hanging out on the beach, and of course I was in the very shallow part where the water only came to my calves and my cousins were in the deep water. While I was minding my own business, a little boy who was about five years old by the name of David approached me. He caught my attention because he was alone but had a floating device. There were a lot of people at the beach that day, and I was shocked his parents were not around.

As David and I engaged in small talk, a huge wave came up that made me stumble and it knocked David over. That made me nervous because I knew I couldn't swim and I did not want to be responsible for a little child while surrounded by all of that water. The look on his face after he was able to stand up, showed me he was terrified. I asked him if he was ok, and his adult answer surprised me. He said, "Yes, ma'am, yes, ma'am. I knew God was going to take care of me." Instantly my spirit began to rejoice, because if this child had enough faith to know that God was going to take care of him, then I knew God would take care of me as well. That time in my life I was unemployed and had to have what I now refer to as "David faith," which means in a life or death situation I have to have faith that God will take care of me no matter what. Years later when things in my life were unsettled and my faith needed a boost, I was again reminded of a child's faith and I was encouraged.

My vacation came to an end, but my job hunts did not. I was released from my job in the middle of April and by that time it was the middle of July. I did not regret losing that job; however, there was some nervousness beginning to set in. I did have some interviews and a couple of people who wanted to hire me, but it was for a door-to-door sales position that would not pay my bills. I had applied for a position at a career school and I was waiting to hear back from them. At the beginning of August, we had a family reunion in Cardinal, Kentucky and I was praying that I would at least get an interview. On the Friday that I arrived, I received a call from the school and they scheduled a phone interview for the following week. The call came while I was at my aunt's house and I started screaming with all of my family there. My thoughts were if I could get an interview, I could get the job. I just needed a chance.

Before my interview I studied the company and the expectations in the job description, so I would be ready. The position was to assist the graduates in finding employment after graduation, which I'd had years of experience doing. When the interviewer called, I answered those questions like I had created them, and she seemed to be impressed. The interview was over, and I was pleased with how it went, but I still had to wait for the next step, which was a face-to-face interview with the director and a tour of the school. Approximately one week after the phone interview, I received my call for the face-to-face interview. Things were looking up and I knew the job God created just for me was around the corner. Whatever God had for me I knew that was exactly what I was going to get, nothing more, nothing less.

My interview was scheduled for the next week, and once again, I nailed it. That was a huge self-esteem booster for me, since I was starting to feel defeated. Following the interview, I had a call from a staffing company that wanted to interview me as well. Yes, I scheduled that one to see if it would be a good fit and I kind of wanted a change in career. As I prepped for the previous interview, I did the same for this one. The morning of the interview, I was nervous but well prepared. If everything went well and I got the job, it would be an adjustment because I had only done nonprofit work, and this was not that. The interview went very well, and once again I was playing the waiting game. I went from not being able to get an interview for a job I wanted, to getting back-to-back interviews. While I waited for the results of the second interview, the first employer wanted to move forward in the hiring process. That was a time I had to go in prayer, because I really wanted the second job, but I had to be realistic. Shortly after seeking God's direction, the second job interviewer called me back and wanted to hire me. I told the career school I was opting to take another position and they were disappointed. My decision to take the staffing job was solely based on prayer and the desire for change.

Things were coming together for my good and working on my behalf. There was a lot of paperwork to fill out and once I completed it, I received my start date. My new position paid more than the previous job, but not what I requested. I was ok with that because it was more. My soon-to-be manager called me about two or three days before I was due to start, and she was very sweet and down to earth. She was encouraging and excited for me to be a part of her team. In all of my positions I have never had a manager call prior to my start date and make sure I was ready to start. Having her call let me know that I would enjoy working for her and the company.

On my first day, naturally I was a little nervous. I got up extra early, got dressed and headed out. The drive was long with morning rush-hour traffic; it took me about an hour to get there and I was punctual. My manager greeted me with a smile and instructions on what to do for the day. She expressed to me that I would train at that location, but then I would be working at the location in Kentucky, not Ohio. The first day was filled with paperwork and training on the computer. The only negative thing was my lack of sleep the night before. The excitement of starting a new job prevented me from sleeping and about halfway through the day I felt it. For the most part the day went really well, and I was looking forward to my new journey.

About two weeks later I was at the Kentucky office and things were great. At the time there was another lady there that would help train me. She was sweet and did assist me with any questions I had. Things were going well, people were getting hired and I was content with the work I was producing. In this position I was able to get out and network at events to recruit employees. One thing I noticed was the manager and my coworker did not have a good relationship, but I stayed neutral and clear of any negative opinions.

That job was very demanding in every way. We were responsible for filling positions with companies, with very little information to pull from. There were days when my coworker and I would stay over late to make sure all jobs were filled. We also were given a company cell phone, so when employees would not show up, the companies would call us any time of the day or night. My coworker became very stressed and it reflected in her work. After only being with the company two months, my coworker was fired. There were only two people in our office: her and me. Her termination was a bit of a shock to me, but I had to move forward.

Christmas is the busiest time of the year for staffing agencies and the volume of help they need is enormous. Since I was still learning the ins and outs of staffing, I knew I had to step up my game, since I was running the office by myself. My manager would come and help when she could, but she was running two offices, so she was stretched as well. In one month I hired over two hundred people alone, so the help was needed. She was able to convince her boss that I needed help, and they finally provided some.

They sent a man who had been in the staffing business for over twenty years and he could not believe I was able to keep up with the volume and demands. He told me once that the work I was doing would take five to six people under any other circumstances. Some days I had to go out and recruit people to work for us, and while I was out at a nonprofit organization, they asked me to come and work for them and let me know they were willing to pay me more than I was making. When I returned to the office, the manager somehow knew they wanted to hire me; although I hadn't said a word, and she told her boss.

Now, when I first got hired I asked for a certain amount and he told me that he could not give me that. Then when he heard another company wanted me, he gave me the amount I originally asked for, along with an additional three thousand dollars. My boss also went to church, so right in her office I broke out in a praise and dance. I was working so hard that the general manager noticed and wanted to give me a bonus of one thousand dollars. He was impressed with my work ethic and wanted to reward me. Jesus will always give you not only what you need, but what you want as well. It amazed me that it took someone else wanting me to come work for them for the manager to understand my true worth. I accepted his offer and chose to stay in that position.

A few weeks after I was told I would be getting the bonus and after everything slowed down, people from other offices came to help. That job became extremely stressful and overwhelming, but I showed up every day and gave one hundred percent. When the "help" showed up, they began to criticize everything that I did and were overbearing and pushy. For the first time in this position I felt uncomfortable and no longer wanted to be there. Yes, there were mistakes found, but I was in the position two months and had to completely take over a full office with minimal help.

Once the smoke cleared everyone wanted to come to the rescue, but where was everyone in the midst of the chaos? Needless to say they found one too many mistakes and I was fired by my sweet manager. When she gave me the news, her eyes were filled with tears and she explained she had no control over the decision. I told her I understood, and I would be okay. Even with this termination I knew that my David faith would kick in and God would once again take care of me.

When I was packing my things to leave, I did not cry or get upset. This time it was different, the shock factor was real since the news had come out of nowhere. I thought I had finally gotten the job down, but when God wants you on another path, He will do just that. Jesus has enough power to shut doors, redirect, and remove you from places where He does not want you. From my own personal life experiences, I recognize He has the power to RIP OFF THE LABELS that prevent us from being free. Yes, this did make me reevaluate who I was and my purpose, but I knew I had to get on the right course. I felt like Jonah in the bible, and how he tried to evade God's will, and even though he tried, God put him in the belly of the whale. There was probably nothing comfortable about being in the whale, but it did get Jonah back on track. Sometimes we have to be uncomfortable to get to where we are going, and as long as we are in God's perfect will, we will be alright. Everything that God has promised you will come to pass, but you must trust Him.

In life it is crucial to have a support system that you can depend on in times when you are weak. During my months of unemployment, my tight circle consisted of my friend from the bank who helped me move, Zakeya, William, Tasha, my cousins Sean and Stephanie, and a couple of people from church. These were the people who stuck with me when I did not wa.0nt to stick with myself—I wanted to throw in the towel. They would always show up right on time with a call, card, or a text to encourage me. Zakeya would tell me at least once a week that God was going to create a job for me. Yes, that sounded good; however, I was not sure if that would ever happen for me. Even though I was unsure, I knew she and Jesus were like best friends and He would often give her insight on things before revealing them to the person with the issue. I did hold on to what she relayed to me, especially in this situation.

I will admit that this time around I became discouraged and low self-esteem set in again. The devil tried to make me believe I was not smart enough and did not deserve to work. Prayer came in handy again and I turned to Jesus as a way to cope. I did not get depressed, but I was discouraged. I continued to apply for jobs and received a phone call from Monarch Youth Services where I had applied two weeks prior. My dream job has always been to work with at-risk youth because I was one and I wanted them to see that they did not have to be a product of their environment. There were two positions open and yes, the ambitious me applied for both of them. When I arrived at the interview, I found that the lady who interviewed me was over both positions I applied for. That was in my favor, because it was kind of like having two interviews in one. During the interview she asked me which position I would want the most, but honestly, it did not matter to me. My interviewer thought with my background and experience that I would be excellent as the admissions counselor, and I was okay with that. I just wanted to be in a position where I was able to flourish and use my testimony to encourage others.

Having two positions end in a matter of seven months would take a toll on anyone. I went from being the best at everything I did, to being the worst at what I did. I did not hear back from Monarch Youth Services, so I decided to clear my head and go to Indiana for a week or two. Ms. Thomas had major surgery on her back and needed some help, so I went to help her and give William a break. It kept me busy and I was able to sit with Ms. Thomas and get wisdom that I could not get anywhere else. We would stay up late talking about life decisions, God, men, and everything in between like two teenage girls. I enjoyed every minute with her. Even though she was in recovery and needed a lot of assistance, her heart and mind were still healthy, and she was just as loving.

Three or four days after I got to Ms. Thomas's, I received a call from Monarch Youth Services confirming that I did get the job and they needed a start date. Being off from work for about a month and a half this time was still too long, I told her I could start on the following Monday which was only four days away. I did not want to leave, but I knew the journey had to continue at home. When I left I could tell Ms. Thomas did not want me to leave either, but she knew I had to as well. It's great to have people in your life that will support you on every level but require nothing in return. The time I spent with Ms. Thomas was so special because for years while in college she fed my friends and me every Sunday for free. There was nothing that we could give her: one, because she had everything she wanted and needed and two, we did not have anything. Having the opportunity to assist her back to health was an honor, especially since she poured so much into me whenever I needed her.

LABEL 33

Instability

Once I returned back home, it was time to start work in two days. I wanted to be ready, so I began searching for my outfit two days prior. I wanted to make sure everything was in order and any obstacles were removed. When Monday arrived, and I woke up to a snow storm, I knew that was not good for my first day. I was excited about the opportunity, so I did not sleep which became my norm when something big was on the horizon. The first thing I did at five in the morning was call my new job to ask if staff still had to come in. Monarch Youth Services is open twenty-four hours a day, seven days a week for three-hundred and sixty-five days a year because it is a residential facility for youth, ages sixteen to twenty-four. The employee who answered explained that they are always open, and I had to come in by any means necessary. When he told me that, I got up immediately and started making my way to my first day on the job.

In my opinion first days are always the same: You spend half of the day filling out paperwork and the other half is spent reading and training. That first day was no different. The lady who was previously in the position trained me and showed me the ropes. In the position as the Intake Coordinator, I was able to observe her interview some of the students who were interested in the program. That day we also did some outreach and visited a homeless shelter where we recruited some of the students. I knew I would enjoy doing that job and was happy my manager realized that position would be a better fit for me. When that day ended, I felt at peace and happy. I felt I was finally in a place where I could flourish.

Things began to flow well, and I was getting the hang of my new position. The students loved me, even though I showed them tough love. Most of the students knew it was for their own good and they respected that. While interviewing students to see if they would be good candidates for our program, they were very transparent with some of their responses. Going into the position, I understood I would be working with students with extreme barriers. Students would share with me experiences I could not believe they had to go through. Some were HIV positive, raped by a family member, some were homeless, and one had not been to school since the seventh grade. At that point in my life I had learned to appreciate all of the things I'd been through, because people survived worse and lived to tell about it. The students began to find a safe haven in my office and congregated in there often.

Many of my students struggled with trusting people because like me, many whom they did trust had betrayed them. The fact that the students trusted me enough to share their innermost secrets and wanted to be around me all of the time said a lot. My students came from a place where failure was their only option and success was a dream that only came a few times a year. When my students entered my office, I not only told them they could have and be anything they wanted regardless of what society had labeled them, but I showed them as well. The biggest testimony you can have is transparency and experience. Most of my students respected and listened to what I said because just a decade and a half prior, I *was* them. I was the student who acted out in class, the one who wanted to make everyone laugh, the one who hid behind hurt, pain, and abuse.

The months passed, and things began to get real. The demands of the job were beginning to get the best of me. Accepting this position, I knew I would have to meet goals and I was okay with that because I am competitive. Meeting goals was not difficult, the difficult part came in when I was being "graded" for the actions of my students. Every time a student left before a certain time, I was graded. All students had to be drug tested to get into the program and if they failed the initial test, they could test again in about a month. The students struggled with smoking marijuana, so they would not pass the second drug test, which led to their termination from the program. All of these barriers affected my performance grade, which made my job stressful. My first year in this position I was ranked number one in the country out of one-hundred-and-twenty-five centers in admissions. Yes, the position was difficult, but I gave all that I had to be successful. When I received the news of my ranking, I rejoiced in knowing that labels are placed but hard work will rip them off.

The second year became more and more tough and the demands increased, and I got tired of dreaming about how many students I needed to reach my monthly goal. That job was beginning to consume my life and it became unhealthy for me. We were in the process of working on a co-enrollment program with a local drop-out credit recovery high school, and since I was the admissions counselor, I was responsible for enrolling the students. The counselor, Ms. Jackson for the high school was a seasoned older white woman who was passive, sweet, knowledgeable, and had a heart for the students. When I first met her, my first thought was how in the world is this lady working with these kids? In my experience, students don't usually respond well to a teacher with her demeanor. After a few visits and encounters with her, she showed me how she did it. Her heart was in it and so was her passion. The students loved her and so did their parents.

Everything was finalized with the co-enrollment program, so I had to begin the interviewing process. Ms. Jackson set up all of the interviews for the students and I went to the school to conduct the interviews. The moment I walked in the building, it just felt right. I liked the atmosphere, and the students seemed well mannered, no different than the students I was already working with. While I was interviewing the students, something told me I should see if there was a position for me there and if they were hiring. I was already looking for other positions and I had a couple of offers and interviews, but nothing seemed to be a good fit for me.

When the interviews were over, I pulled the counselor to the side in her office and asked questions about the school and the vision. She knew exactly where I was going with it and waited patiently for my talkative self to finish. I was nervous about asking about a position due to her building a relationship with my current boss and the director of the organization. Before the words could leave my mouth, she took me straight to the principal and told him all about me and said that he should hire me. She explained to him that she had watched me conduct orientations, and how I interacted with the students. Orientation was my favorite part of the job, because I love public speaking and it allowed me to speak in front of a group.

He seemed to be impressed and told me about a position that he was thinking about creating and that he thought I would be a good fit. I told him I did not have a teaching degree and he was okay with that. The principal scheduled me for an interview for the following week. When I left the school, I was in shock from all that had just taken place. You never know who is watching you, so always give your best at everything; it could lead to your next blessing.

The moment I got into my vehicle, I called Zakeya to tell her that what she told me about a job that was created for me had just happened. She was so excited and kept saying, "See, I told you. I knew God would create a job for you." That took place in October and all of the details needed to be worked out, so I knew it would take some time. I was in a place where I wanted to be, happy and at peace. When you have given all you can give, but it is not enough, it's time to move on. The position that I was currently in was good, and I loved my students, but the demand was too much. I showed up every day, rarely missing work and did an excellent job for the company and my students.

Two months rolled by and I kind of forgot about the job at the high school because we could not agree on the salary. While I was still doing the admissions counselor duties, the school counselor emailed me and then called me to let me know she was still working on a position for me. She expressed that she was so impressed with me and she felt I would be a great asset to the school. That blew my mind and I thought, this lady does not even know me but was standing in the gap, speaking on my behalf. God has a way of making your character speak for you even in your absence.

Time was still rolling by and I had not heard from the principal, so I just put it out of my mind and continued working. I figured if that job was for me, then I would get it and it would be an easy, peaceful transition. In February on a Sunday morning while I was sitting in church, I received a call from a number I did not recognize, so I let it go to voicemail. Later that night after night service, I decided to listen to the message, and lo and behold it was Ms. Jackson, the school counselor. One thing I can say about her is she was persistent and full of tenacity. I called her that night and she wanted me to know that she was still pulling for me and that I should be hearing something soon. Ms. Jackson told me she reminded the principal about me a few times a week and jokingly she added, "I think he thinks we are related, because I remind him so much."

Her word was true. The principal called me later that week and wanted me to come in again to revisit the position he had opened. Upon arriving to the interview, I remained positive and in good spirits. At the time of the interview, the main concern was the salary that he was willing to pay. Not one time did he question my ability to do the job, which meant he trusted

Ms. Jackson's recommendation. We finally came to an agreement about my salary and he offered me the position right on the spot. The principal explained to me that I would get spring break, two months in the summer, two weeks in the winter, and all of the national holidays off. When he finished telling me the days I would have off, he added that they would all be paid. That was the best paid time off ever. I would work three months less, and my checks would not change. He asked if I could start on the following Monday, and I explained to him that I needed to give my current job two weeks' notice. The principal understood my request and gave me my start date for two weeks out. Everything that I ever wanted in a job was given to me in just one meeting.

The time came when I had to give my two-week notice at the current job, and in all honesty, I got emotional about it. Before I turned it in, I told my boss and the center director about it and both of them were excited for me. I expected them to have a different reaction, but surprisingly it was supportive. The hard part was telling my students about my new job. The students who were close to me I brought into my office and told them. The frustration, anger, and tears began to flow, they were so upset with me. Even though I knew I was in the will of God, the students were making me second guess my decision. They were mad at me and said things like, "Ms. Percy, you're going to love them kids and not us?" "How are you just going to leave us?" "Ms. Percy, this is not fair." Every time a student would say something like that to me, I would have to hold back the tears. I had to remember that God's will triumphs over everything and everyone, even me.

What I did not tell a lot of people was that as much as the students needed me, I needed them more. That position was not just for the students; it was for me. There were many days when I came in and life just happened, and I needed a smile, a joke, or something to pick me up and then in came a student who made me feel better. The position allowed me to be transparent and share with the students the labels that were placed on me and how I was able to rip them off. Looking at a person on the outside does not always show the truth about what that individual is going through. Strength is something that comes from lifting the heavy loads that life brings. It makes us strong and allows us to move forward.

My last day at Monarch Youth Services I was sick with the flu, but still managed to get my office packed up and get to the doctor. The week before, I was extremely overwhelmed with all of the transition that was taking place, but my wonderful coworkers helped me greatly. They encouraged me, comforted me, and even told me to shake it off and get it together. I am currently working at a high school that I absolutely love, and where I am able to make a difference. My heart has so much love for the youth that I continued working at Monarch Youth Services even after I got another job.

In retrospect, I can look back and naturally ask Jesus why things happened the way they happened. However, when things were fast forwarded to the present, it all makes sense. Labels can be given to us to push us to our dreams, our destiny, and our future. Any label that has been attached to me, I've found the strength to rip off during the pain and heartache. I can operate in my purpose and be who and what God says I am, and you have the same strength residing on the inside. Once you rip off the labels other people have placed on you, next you must rip off the labels you've put on yourself. When you label yourself, it is more detrimental to you and your growth as a person due to your reflection in the mirror daily. However, when society labels you, in most cases, you have the ability to walk away and never face them again.

Stop labeling yourself and live beyond what you think you are. The only labels we must accept are the labels that God has put on us and any other positive labels. Every day when you get up, tell yourself that you are beautiful, smart, wanted, and most of all, loved. Many days I found myself in tears because I felt unwanted and unloved; however, even if it's just one person in this world, I can promise you that you make the difference in someone's life. There is at least one person who is depending on your strength, courage, love, and support to rip off the labels in their life.

If you notice that throughout my life, God has always strategically placed people that supported me. These individuals are what I would like to call my cheerleaders. My cheerleaders would cheer for me when I was losing and wanted to forfeit. They cheered for me when I was injured mentally and emotionally and had to sit on the side lines. I even received their encouragement when the opposing team bullied and mocked me because of my failures. There were many people who came to the game when I was on a winning streak, but did not invest in me when I lost. My cheerleaders showed up at their appointed times and endured the pain that came with the ripping process. Most of the labels that will be ripped off primarily is all on the person that needs to be label free. However, be mindful that you need cheerleaders. Cheerleaders will not always be who you think like family, for me it was teachers, friends, coworkers, and other people that God sent. Every stage in my life, my cheerleaders grew, not a lot, but enough to get me to the next level. God reminded me that he would never leave me nor forsake me, so he will make sure someone is there to stand in the gap. Everybody will not be a part of our cheer squad, so when allowing people in make sure they have your best interest at heart. Please be aware that the people who will be a part of your cheer team may not look like you think they should. My cheerleaders are comprised of men, women, older, younger, black, white, educated, wealthy, and other opposites than myself. Embrace the love that they must give, appreciate their support, and don't push them away due to your own insecurities. We are not an island; a group of cheerleaders is essential for ripping off the labels.

I have a great friend who reminds me often, no matter what is going on, that it will all work out, and everything will be okay. Just like you who are reading this, I struggle with labels every day, but I refuse to let them define who I am and restrict me from walking in my purpose and destiny. The most valuable thing that I have learned throughout my life is every label starts as a seed; it's up to us whether we water it or let it die. Once a seed is planted it grows roots, and those roots make it difficult to uproot, but just know you are strong enough to RIP THE LABELS OFF.

About the Author

Ryda Isabella Percy is a fun, energetic, and outgoing individual who loves public speaking. Ryda enjoys inspiring, empowering, encouraging, and motivating people to walk in their purpose. She grew up in Indiana, where she attended the University of Liberal Arts and received her bachelor's degree in Interpersonal Communications. Although society has counted her out numerous times and put labels on her, Ryda has found strength to rip those labels off and live life to the fullest. Through her faith in Jesus, she has learned how to survive difficult times. Currently, Ryda works at an inner city high school with primarily at-risk youth and specializes in drop out credit recovery. Ryda resides in Kentucky with her dog Prince. *Rip the Labels Off* is her first book.

CPSIA information can be obtained
at www.ICGtesting.com
Printed in the USA
FFHW02n1322310818
48181566-51901FF